# Fight to
# Make it Happen

## 6 Power Principles to Fulfilling Your Purpose & Living Your Dreams

# Tonya D. Breland

TESO Publishing

TONYA BRELAND

ISBN-13: 978-0692552292 (TESO Publishing)

ISBN-10: 0692552294

## DEDICATION

I want to dedicate this book first to my loving, supportive husband, Gerard...you put it on the screen and you made it happen...faith and works!  I also want to dedicate this book to my children, Gianya and Daniel.  As you discover your purpose, my prayer is that you will go after your dreams and live life to the full.  I love you all very much.

# CONTENTS

# ACKNOWLEDGMENTS

*Writing this book has been a dream come true for me. I have enjoyed writing since I was a little girl. For decades, I have had a desire to write a book that would add value to adults and I'm so happy I finally made it happen. It could not have happened without the inspiration and support of so many. I have to first give thanks to God, who has gifted me in so many ways. He has positioned me to be able to* **Make it Happen** *in my life and help others* **Make it Happen.**

*I dedicated this book to my husband and children, but I must acknowledge them further. Gerard has been nothing short of supportive through this and many many other endeavors. He believed from the first real conversation I had with him that I could be and do whatever I desired and he has pushed and supported me every step of the way. My children are on their own journeys of self-discovery and I believe they will accomplish great things in their lives. I pray they are never afraid to* **Make it Happen** *because they are both so gifted, talented and intelligent. I love them tremendously and can't wait to see what God has in store for them.*

*I must also acknowledge my parents, all of them. In many ways, I am so much like my father, as he has written numerous books. I don't always realize how much I follow in his footsteps, but I'm happy to. I thank him and my (step) mother for raising me, loving me and supporting me. My mother and late (step) father have always been so proud and supportive of everything I do...that means a lot to me. I love you. I must also honor the memory of my grandparents, Theodore & Ernestine Smith, who were my biggest champions. They set such an outstanding example for me and they were both so gifted, loving, generous and supportive. I miss them dearly. I know they'd be proud.*

*I thank God for great girlfriends who are supportive, keep me laughing, moving forward and energetic. Everybody needs friends like you ladies. I love ya'll...Tinky (my sista), Damaris (my girl), Paige (my accountability partner), Michaelle (my ride or die), Monica (my friend 'til death), Lori (my inspiration), Deborah (my soul-sister) Daniela (my supporter) & Joy (my "FRIEND"). I also have a host of other friends and family members who I cannot name. You know who you are...I love you all.*

*I want to also acknowledge my first mentee, Taribah. You are an awesome young woman who I am so proud of. You know I love you!*

*I must also acknowledge, Carla Jones, my editor and friend. Remember her name. She is a genius. I know very many intelligent and wonderful people, but Carla is by far one of the most intelligent. She is well read and a remarkable writer. Plus she's a good friend. Her vocabulary is so extensive, she makes me look up words in the dictionary. I* cannot express enough how much I appreciate your "editorialization" (inside joke). You willingly accepted the challenge as I made myself vulnerable to your scrutiny, but we did it! You are amazing and without you, **"Fight to Make it Happen"** would still be a work in progress.

I must also acknowledge Evergreen Ave. School and my former teaching staff who helped Make it Happen for students and trusted me to lead as their principal. I will always have fond memories of my experience there and how you contributed to them. Thank you.

I want to acknowledge Brittnee (Bynoe) Smith. Remember her name too...she is my trusted assistant and protégé . She is so talented. She is the creator of my book cover, website and so much more. Great things are in store for her. Thank you, "Girl on the Right" for making me look good.

Last but not least, my Destiny Family with Pastors Jonathan & Kamili. You all are a blessing to the people whose lives you touch. Thank you for touching mine and for your unending support. Love all of you Leaths!

# 1 INTRO

"If money were no object, how would you live your life differently?" Those words rang loudly in my ear and kept replaying in my mind over and over again, like a broken record as I sat in the audience that night. It was as though I was the only listener. No one else seemed to matter in that moment as I repeated those words in my head. *What would I do? What would be different?* In other words, if I could have chosen to do absolutely anything I wanted to do, without worrying about money, what would that be? Why am I even on this earth and why did God create me?

It was the year 2002 when I worked as an elementary teacher. I had been in a car accident and was on disability leave recovering from neck and back injuries. The young boy who hit my car from behind could not stop the car quickly enough and when I looked in my rearview mirror and saw his car approaching quickly, I braced myself for the inevitable impact. The car didn't sustain major damage, but I endured enough to alter my life.

My injuries were confined to my neck and back in the form of soft tissue damage, herniated cervical discs, lower back disc harm as well as nerve problems with my left arm. For the next 6 months, I experienced muscle spasms from the shoulders down to my lower extremities that made it very uncomfortable for me to sit, stand, or lie down. It seemed no position was helpful. The muscle relaxers helped somewhat because they usually put me to sleep so that I didn't have to feel any pain, but that meant I was stuck at home convalescing. I couldn't drive under the influence of those meds. I alternated between Ibuprofen and the prescribed anti-inflammatory pills that I tried to avoid taking because of the side effects. I tried to manage without them, growing more and more accustomed to the tingly, throbbing sensation that travelled from my neck to the fingertips of my left arm. It was as though I was continually hitting the "funny bone", but there was no laughter coming from me.

I began to look forward to the weekly physical therapy sessions because I knew I would at least get some relief from the neck, back and shoulder adjustments of the therapist. In between therapy sessions, I had to practice neck exercises designed to lessen the pain over time. There was a lot of talk back and forth with the doctor about whether I would need surgery to help in the recovery process and this made me anxious. Fortunately, I managed to escape the surgery, but it would be six months before I experienced a day without pain.

The things I previously took for granted like cooking, walking up and down the stairs, standing from a sitting position, bending and lifting were now chores for me. I could barely stand up straight to walk and my young children needed to help me walk from the house to the car. They gingerly held my arm as I walked up the stairs and they provided balance for me when I transitioned from sitting to standing. It reminded me of when I was a young child helping my great-grandmother with her mobility. She was disabled and it was difficult for her to move from point A to point B without assistance. Now it was me being given the assistance. "You walk like an old lady," one of my kids impatiently proclaimed as they waited for me to move from one place to the next. It was awful. I was still a young, vibrant woman, at least that's how I saw myself in my own head, yet my movements and the occasional use of a cane suggested otherwise. The school district would not let me return to work until I was medically cleared without restrictions and so I spent those 6 months recovering and mending from the chronic, constant pain. This left me with plenty of time to think and evaluate where I was in my life. Over time, the pain became much more manageable and I was able to return to some of the things I enjoyed doing. Although I was not fully recovered, I was very determined to continue living my life.

The night I attended that special event, I felt like I was living again. For once, my injuries took a back seat. Meds and a heating pad took care of that. I was tired of feeling like I was incapacitated and my life was on hold. I was mentally ready for a change and that's when the fighter in me pushed to the forefront. My husband and I attended this event as invited guest singers. I might have suffered injuries, but nothing was wrong with my singing voice and so I continued to accept invitations to sing, even if it meant I had to sing sitting down or wearing my heating pad.

The evening involved other invited guests, including the speaker who made an impression on me when she described how she was living the life of her dreams. She was energetic, charismatic and she smiled an awful lot. Something about her made me take notice. She confidently stood and declared to the audience that she was there to change lives. She told her story of how she had been in corporate America, enjoying a life of measurable success, but she was not fulfilled with her corporate life. *She was living the American dream! What's not fulfilling about that?* (I thought to myself.) I think her story really prompted me to listen more intently. I had never met anyone like her. Deep down inside I was searching for more fulfillment in my own life and hearing her brought that desire to the surface.

It's not uncommon to be in a job or career and come to a point in life where you begin to question who you are, where you are going and what you are doing. You may find yourself reevaluating your aspirations and dreams and even measuring your progress in reaching them. You may begin searching beyond what you're presently doing to find what you think might be missing or needed to fill the void. That night was the beginning of my search for more, albeit it was somewhat happenstance and unplanned. I didn't know that I would be hearing her message and I certainly had no idea how poignant her message would be to me. This encounter was divinely orchestrated. It was not a coincidence for me to be there at that particular time. This woman's presentation spoke to questions I held buried inside of me. And although I didn't quite know where this night would lead, I always believed things happen in life for a reason and one day, I would see the full picture.

She went on to share how her life was changed when she attended an event and met a woman who seemed to have found happiness and fulfillment by running and operating her own business. The speaker continued with her story and I soon realized she was ultimately pushing that very same business on her audience of listeners. And for some odd reason, I was mesmerized by her, business and all. Something about her resonated with me. Truthfully, she was pushing how to find a life of fulfillment, but she was clothing it in her line of business. As she continued talking, she made it obvious that she was looking for people, women in particular, who were interested in changing their circumstances. She was talking to me. She was offering an opportunity for everyone to do business with her or simply just earn a little extra money. I secretly wanted what she was offering. I wanted a change. I wanted something different to happen in my life and I was willing to take a risk and follow her. And the timing could not have been better. That car accident was a blessing in disguise.

Many times events occur that seemingly interrupt what we are doing. Those events are unpredictable, sometimes traumatic, sometimes irritating, and other times simply life changing and we cannot control them. We just have to respond to them and make decisions about how to navigate them. It's often unexpected, shocking and uncomfortable, but don't rule out the blessing of these life changing events. Though they are difficult, challenging and sometimes problematic, they can be exactly what you need to refocus your life and your circumstances. Once you get over the emotional impact, you then have an opportunity to reassess your values and position in life. Treasure these opportunities, they do not happen all of the time. My car accident was that event for me. I'm glad I used it as an opportunity.

That evening as I was listening to the woman present, she was influencing me in ways that I could not have predicted.

Because of her and the timing of the accident, I was going to make something new happen in my life, something that would ultimately impact my life and the lives of others for many years to come. I didn't know the lady yet, but she had a way of making things happen for herself and for others and although I didn't plan it, she was going to show me how she did it and eventually I would follow suit. What I was not yet able to see was how these life changing events were connected to my overall purpose. Try not to underestimate certain events and experiences; they may be more significant than you realize. That's a lesson I continue to learn.

Sometimes I wish I could go back in time and explain to my younger, more naïve self how important it is to understand ourselves and the experiences that lead to discovering who we are and how our decisions impact our purpose. Fortunately for me, this decision to follow the woman positively impacted me. It filled a void that I didn't even know I had at the time. Don't get me wrong, my teaching career was enjoyable and I felt I was making a difference, but something inside of me made me feel like there was more waiting for me in life.

Teaching was a means to an end, but I had no idea what that end looked like. I just felt that the difference I was making in the classroom could be expanded, but I didn't have clarity about it yet. You may be able to identify with feeling somewhat empty or unfulfilled while wishing and praying that something would change to open your eyes to the path for you to go in a different direction. Whatever that is, is already inside of you, put there before you were conceived. Everybody has a purpose and everybody has a path they are supposed to take in life. Sometimes it takes a lifetime to discover it and sometimes it takes an event, like a car accident.

I wasn't really all that interested in the products that the lady was selling that night, but I found myself drawn to her message and hanging onto her every word. She wasn't promoting her product, she was promoting her lifestyle. I was so impressed that when the event was over, I found myself standing at the front of the room, like others in the audience, anxiously waiting to talk to her, though not sure what to say. It was as though I was having a "come to Jesus" experience and she was the preacher waiting for me at the altar. The only thing missing was the tears. I approached her with questions about her business and expressed an interest in doing something I'd never imagined myself doing. Not only was I making a change in my life, but I was becoming an Independent Beauty Consultant! What was I thinking? Sure, it was a well-established company and sure, I could, "earn a few extra dollars," but what was I really signing up to do? The irony of all of this is that I was a minimalist when it came to wearing make-up, and of course make-up was a major component to being a beauty consultant. Yet, I was still joining. This was going to be an interesting ride. My decision led to the warmest embrace by the speaker. She pulled me in close enough for me to smell her signature scent and promised to help make my dreams come true, *whatever they were.*

It was apparent that lady was living her dream life. She had left the safety and comfort of a cushy executive position and she was doing something that seemed to bring her great joy and satisfaction. I couldn't quite understand how being a beauty consultant could bring so much joy, but I was missing the big picture. It wasn't about the products, it was about the personal satisfaction and empowerment that was gained. Who knew how this decision was supposed to help me fulfill my own dreams? Certainly not me, but I was about to find out.

Sometimes during your journey, you may go down a road that doesn't seem to be in the right direction, but find out that there are some wonderful pit stops and shopping areas filled with all kinds of special goodies for you. I had to trust that inner small voice inside of me that whispered, "It's okay to take this path. I've got some surprises for you. Don't worry, you'll see how it leads back to the main road in no time." Listen to the guiding voice inside of you that prompts you to go down a new unpredictable path. That voice for me is the voice of God. I've never been led astray by listening to and following God's voice.

The decision to become a beauty consultant was definitely out of my element. But there was something about taking this step that night that seemed right. This was very different for me, and turned out not to be a bad decision. I would later discover just how much this decision was going to have a tremendous impact on the rest of my life. (We'll talk more about this later.) I was taking a step toward a dream, although to the outsider looking in, I was signing up to be a beauty consultant. You could say that this peculiar move was a blind act of faith. I had no idea what was ahead for me and I didn't really care, but I trusted the move because of my faith. It felt right.

When I signed up to be a beauty consultant, it was almost like impulse buying. It only cost me $100 and based on the description by the presenter, it sounded like I could earn that back in no time at all. I confess I didn't quite have a grasp on what I was signing up for, but I was intrigued by the promise of earning extra money and deep down inside the promise of making my dreams come true, whatever that meant. The more I learned about my new role, the more I laughed internally. Who was I to advise anybody on wearing make-up? This was going to be an interesting adventure for me. In hindsight, I was taking a step that would put me in a position to do what I was put on this earth to do...empower and inspire people to reach their God-given potential, that is to make a difference. I wish I could have appreciated every moment of it back then, but you know what they say, "Hindsight is 20/20."

Everyone is put here on this earth for a reason, a purpose. Sometimes we know what it is, other times we spend years searching for it. What's most interesting is that our purpose or mission, as others would call it, is a part of who we are at our core. It's always been in us, even as early as our childhood. Unfortunately, most people have no idea what their purpose is, why they're here and what they're supposed to do. We settle for things we can do, rather than what we're purposed to do and we miss the mark and therefore miss out on living the most fulfilling lives we can and deserve to live. Your purpose is your why, your life's mission, why you were placed here on this earth.

I lived for years unconscious to my purpose, though it was always inside of me and even made appearances at different key times. In fact, it made appearances all the time, but like I said, I didn't even know it. I was oblivious to it until recently. One day a friend of mine decided to write a tribute to me and other women who have impacted her life and she wrote that I was her "Make it happen" friend. It was hard at first for me to conceptualize what she was saying, but it really resonated within. I grappled with the "Make it Happen" concept and mulled it around in my head for a while and began to understand what she had long seen in me. She saw my purpose being lived out through our friendship. She saw me as a person who pushed to make things happen in life, and she saw my purpose behind my making things happen.

Ultimately, I was peeling back the layers of me and my actions over the span of my life and I was discovering a lot about myself. It took me having to see it through my friend's eyes first, but what she was seeing was a woman who was placed here on this earth to help empower, inspire and encourage others to find their passion and live up to their God-given potential, someone who was here to make a difference in the lives of others. It was the "why" behind my signing up to become a beauty consultant, not the products I was selling. My friend knew this because she had been on a similar journey when she also signed up to be a beauty consultant. I just couldn't see and appreciate my purpose yet.

# 2 WHY AM I HERE?

I stepped out on faith and tried the new business that at another time in my life would have been easily dismissed. The business didn't quite fit my idea of "career" and it certainly didn't fit into any of the plans or dreams I had for myself nor the dreams my parents had for me. After all, they sent me to college to do something "meaningful" and "productive" and being a teacher was more like that "something." Little did I know how much my decision to sell make-up would change the trajectory of my life forever. This unique, out of the box experience would prove to be a great example of how I fought to make things happen while exercising some very important principles. It would also prove to be life changing.

I've always been a woman of strong convictions and I believe everyone has a destiny and purpose, although I didn't quite know mine during that stage of my life. I was in my early 30's, searching and knowing deep down inside that there was more I wanted out of my life. I couldn't quite imagine how selling make-up would open up that door of enlightenment for me, but time would reveal more. That woman, my former Sales Director often spoke publicly and never failed to ask people what they wanted out of life. Each time I would hear her, I would find myself dreaming. I would often allow my mind to take me to places of what could be if I did whatever I wanted to do or felt I was called to do. I wasn't even really sure what I wanted, but I liked the idea of having the freedom to dream and to allow my mind to wander. I also spent a lot of time praying about it as a part of my seeking and exploring.

Sometimes my sales director would throw out another question that would cause me to dream, "What would I do if I knew I couldn't fail?" Essentially, this question was asking me to do something that we sometimes take for granted, that is to dream and imagine what could be without the barrier of failure. Allowing myself to dream answered the "how" question of my existence. Once I could figure out why I'm here, my purpose, then I can dream of how I want to live out my purpose.

The truth is, there was nothing wrong with being an educator. I enjoyed working with children and helping them realize their potential, but for some reason, it was not enough for me. I was not completely fulfilled doing this. I had always felt there was more for me to do. In fact, at the time, I was actually enrolled in a Master's program for educational leadership.

Maybe going into educational leadership would fill that space. Interestingly, at the same time, there was a part of me that liked the idea of being an entrepreneur/business owner and this new move in my life opened up the possibilities. If the truth were told, being a beauty consultant was not my first attempt at the business world. Almost a decade prior, I had my first stab at business when I started a non-profit organization. I was only in my 20's at the time with limited work experience and an underdeveloped dream. Ultimately, the non-profit didn't succeed, but the lessons were plentiful and failing didn't make me feel like a failure; I used it as an opportunity to learn and grow. This particular failure helped me to grow in many ways. It also helped me to continue to dream. And dreaming is what I did too. Dreaming is not a one-time thing. If it were, then when we climb to the top of the mountain that we have been dreaming to reach, what would happen next? We would have to come down. And then we have to create new dreams.

In between these two ventures, I also founded a small record label for my husband and me to record our music. As a singer, I even entertained the thought of pursuing music on a professional level. However, for me, music was still mostly a hobby that although I enjoyed doing it, I was never fully invested in making it a profession. My husband, on the other hand, would have probably loved it at one point in our lives. I just wanted to continue to love it. Although I was actively pursuing these other ventures/dreams, I still had not figured out what I was destined to become or do.

There was something inside of me that made me believe I could do all of these things, start businesses, teach, earn a Master's degree in administration, even if I didn't always succeed, as in the case of the non-profit because ultimately, I was on my way to discovering my "why". These dreams were all a part of my journey, the journey that I will share with you as we focus on making things happen in your life, using key principles that will lead you towards your purpose.

From time to time I may ask you to go through some exercises in this book that will guide you through the process of finding your purpose or identifying your dreams. To start, I want you to think about how you would respond to the two weighty questions: if money were no object and if you knew you couldn't fail. What answers come to mind for you? When I considered these questions, I challenged my thinking further by asking myself some pointed questions like, *"What would I do? What could I do? What would I want to do?"* You can ask yourself the same questions. Depending on what you have going on in your life, these questions can be tough to think about and answer. To respond to these questions, you may feel you need a better understanding of who you are and why you are here. I guess you could imagine yourself doing certain things, but it may be harder to do when you are unaware of your purpose for being here. You could easily say, if money were no object, you would travel all around the world. While that may be a fun thing to do and it may be a desire of yours, how does it touch the surface of your destiny? Does it give a clue as to what you value? Is it really something you feel you must do? If it is simply a fun thing to try, maybe you need to look deeper.

This purpose finding process is not a simple matter. It can cause you to feel like you're going in circles for years until you can begin to draw some connections and see patterns in your life's choices and in the short and long term dreams you've had for yourself. You might even be able to tie some of your life decisions to childhood dreams and desires as well as the things you highly value. Don't rush this process. It's very important. Your purpose will be confirmed over and over again in many different ways by your own self-reflection as well as other people's observations of you.

Whenever I engage in the process of reflection related to my purpose, I have to quiet my spirit for a period and really focus and hone in on who I really am, what I really value, what I'm good at doing and what I really want to accomplish. I have to still the noise of the thoughts of who others want me to become and what others want me to do and focus in on what I know deep down inside. I have to push through my own preconceived notions about success and find my truest self.

Usually, I do this with pen and paper. I find that when I write, I release thoughts and open my mind to think more deeply. Begin by writing your values, what you're good at doing, what brings you great joy, what you could see yourself doing if you didn't have to worry about money or failure. This exercise, if done honestly, is very revealing and unlocks those innermost thoughts you carry about yourself. When you're truly honest, you're exposing yourself to your innermost self. You're being fully transparent and open about what beliefs you hold, about what you can actually, realistically accomplish in your life. Your vulnerabilities and fears are exposed to your conscious mind and you need to be willing to accept what's really inside of you and be willing to address it. This exercise, when done carefully and perhaps over a period of time can also be very cathartic. Whenever I've fully delved into my psyche in this way, I discover something new and insightful. I recommend you take some time to do this work. You can also use our **Fight To Make it Happen Handbook,** it will walk you through this process. You can order it on my TonyaBreland.com website.

If I were sitting with you, I would ask you what you have always dreamed of doing and/or becoming. I would ask you questions regarding your earliest memories of your aspirations. I would ask you about what makes you feel alive and fully engaged. I would want to know what deeply interests you and then I would ask you a bunch of whys to help you search within yourself for answers. Sometimes the answers aren't on the surface and take time to discover. I would help you in the discovery process so that you can pinpoint what would make you feel fulfilled and begin carving out a path to find it and walk in it.

Since I'm not sitting with you, I need you to do some of this work on your own. I still want to ask you to consider the questions...what would you do if money were no object or what would you do if you knew you couldn't fail? Allow yourself to dream and dream deeply and sincerely. Don't just settle for the surface thoughts. Spend some quality time searching deep within yourself to uncover who you really are. Take time now to do this work and then come back to the book after you have some answers.

What I like about these questions is they can indirectly dispel common fears people hold...the fear of failing and the fear of not having security and stability. Fear is an obstacle for many people, oftentimes insurmountable and even paralyzing. If the big barrier of fear is removed, there's less to stand in the way of discovering one's destiny. So take some time to allow your mind to wander into places unknown or buried and dream of what could be.

If you are looking to make changes in your business, the exercise is still valuable. Your personal development may give you great insight into why your business is or is not succeeding. If you are doing more of what others expect from you rather than what you're really most passionate about doing, you may not see nor feel complete gratification. You may need to make some changes. This reflective exercise may be just what you need to give you greater insight into what your focus should be in your business.

At many different points in my life, I've done the same thing I'm asking you to do. I dared to dream too for my personal life as well as how it related to my small business. As I dreamed, I thought about what could be different in my life both personally and professionally. I also thought about how much satisfaction I could gain from pondering these deep questions. This process of allowing my mind to engage in this way is actually very stimulating. Dreaming allowed me to explore other options without barriers. There's something almost magical about dreaming which is why we're going to focus on dreaming in the next chapter of this book.

As I dreamed in those early years, my dreams inevitably centered around the issue of what would make me feel fulfilled, vis-à-vis, my purpose, which I was still in the process of searching. That's actually what I hope happens for you. I hope your dreams lead you to your purpose, your place of fulfillment. For me, at the time, I imagined what it would be like to be financially secure, to be able to be more present as a mother to my young children, and the new feats I could accomplish professionally. I thought about my desire to write a book, record music and God only knows what else. My dreams since then have evolved, but the process of dreaming started early. The benefit of starting early is so you can go back and start all over again (when you desire) with new dreams. There are no rules when it comes to dreaming. And by the way, eventually I was able to stay home with my children for a little while, I did record a CD with my husband and I've written one children's chapter book and started several others. Dreams really do and can come true. But I want to caution you to not limit yourself when it comes to dreaming. Dreams can constantly change, but your purpose will likely stay pretty constant. You can achieve many dreams and still not be walking in purpose. Find your purpose so your dreams have more meaning.

So as you begin doing the work to find your purpose and discover your dreams, pay attention to your mindset. What you believe is very critical to what can occur for you. We are going to spend time looking at the beliefs you hold about yourself and your future. I have a very strong faith system and believe if I could dream something, I could certainly achieve it, especially when it is tied to my overall destiny or purpose. Quite honestly this is true for you too. If you have a dream to do something differently in life, why aren't you achieving it? Why aren't you living and going after it? If it's because you don't yet know the "why" behind your existence, don't worry.

I'll help you with this.

Dreaming of your ideal life or business can be overwhelming. It's easy to allow fear to keep you from making the necessary moves towards living the life of your dreams. Many people, actually most adults are afraid of change and are inclined to take the safe route in life because they fear the unknown. They are not sure if the road they choose will indeed lead to the outcome they desire. The unknown road could take them someplace that makes them feel incompetent, insecure, unsuccessful, stressed or unhappy. This is risky. Although the unknown may be scary, embracing the possibilities of the unknown being a happy, safe, secure, successful place makes you adjust your mindset. When I was working as an independent beauty consultant, I used to frequently tell my team that fear is *False Evidence Appearing Real*. You have to decide not to fear, at least that's what I do when fear plops its ugly head into mine. I ask myself what is there to fear, and then I go to work to prove fear wrong and make room for faith.

Either you have one or the other. Faith is when you take the steps towards fulfilling your potential, even though you cannot see how things will turn out. Faith is about taking a risk and knowing that everything will work out. And whatever goes wrong can be viewed and used as a learning experience rather than a failure that stops you from moving forward.

Faith is about looking at what's in your belief system and believing and deciding that you can accomplish what you set out to do.

Our mindset is very powerful. Stanford University professor of Psychology, Dr. Carol Dweck writes extensively about mindset. We either have a fixed mindset or a growth mindset. The growth mindset looks at the possibilities and makes moves believing all the while that this dream is possible. The one with the fixed mindset is quick to throw their hands up in the air as a symbol of surrendering and giving up! The person with the fixed mindset won't even explore the possibilities because his/her mind is already made up that they cannot succeed at doing something new or different. These are the people who don't realize that if you keep doing the same thing the same way, you'll get the same results. Didn't Einstein say that was the definition of insanity? This book was written to help you address your mindset as you fight to make it happen in your life.

Throughout this book, we are going to look at six principles that I've lived by in my life, even before I knew I was being governed by them. They will serve as tenets for you to follow as you pursue your dreams and live the life you want to live or accomplish the goals you set out to accomplish. I want you to realize the greatness in you and the power you wield just by dreaming a dream and doing the work to fulfill it.

I call these keys my "6 Make it Happen Power Principles". I will share lessons from life's stories and how I used these principles throughout the journey to make things happen in my life that ultimately lead to fulfillment. If you are looking for fulfillment in your life, in your relationships, in your career or in your business, this book is for you.

As you read, you will learn how the following principles have changed my life.

1. Dream

2. Live by Faith

3. Build Strong Relationships

4. Be Determined

5. Develop a Plan

6. Fight

# 3 DREAM

"I do not envy you, Tonya! There's no way I could do your job! Whew!" And with that they would usually leave my office, walk away wiping their brow and shaking their heads back and forth, overwhelmed by the very thought of my job. This would tickle me because my job was so far outside of their purpose. I knew as clearly as they that my job was not something they would ever dream of doing or becoming. And luckily for them, nobody was asking them to. These statements were commonly spoken from different teachers I supervised when I served as their principal. They could never imagine or dream of being the principal of the school. The responsibilities were just not what they were accustomed to doing as classroom teachers, nor did they ever want to. They simply could not fathom what it would be like to switch places with me. I understood exactly why they would never aspire to that role. It was never their dream, their calling or desire. They were doing exactly what they were supposed to be doing. They were in their lanes.

Not everyone is so fortunate. Sure, they are doing meaningful work and they may even be living the life others envy, but they know that deep down inside, they are not in their lane. They are not living the life of their dreams. For some, that life doesn't even seem attainable, for others there is a longing for it, and for another group of people, they have no idea what their dreams are. Still there are those who desire to live their dreams, but are afraid. Where are you on this continuum? Are you living the life of your dreams? Chances are if you are reading this book, you may be on the journey, either at the beginning in search of your dreams or at the brink of making some moves in your life to finally live your dreams. Where ever you find yourself on the continuum, you are not alone.

For centuries people have been in search of the meaning of life. Just Google it and you'll find, from Solomon in the Bible to Ralph Waldo Emerson to Einstein to Martin Luther King, Jr., information on the subject. Most people have a longing deep down inside to find out why they were placed here. Some search their whole lives and others become aware after living a little and coming to a crossroads. I have two questions for you: If you're not living your dreams, what's stopping you? And if you desire to live your dreams, what's driving you?

I've spent years trying to figure out my path, praying and seeking, seeking and praying. I've got journals that date back to 2004 filled with ideas and thoughts on the subject only to discover who I am and what I'm supposed to do has always been inside of me, although it has evolved. Each step of my journey had a purpose related to my future. Experience revealed an unfolding of who I am and who I am supposed to be. Who I am today is not who I was yesterday or last year for that matter. Life builds upon itself and experiences are meant for different purposes. My dreams of yesteryear are not necessarily my dreams of today, but all are connected to my purpose and why God placed me here.

I discovered years ago that I was born to make a difference in the lives of others. I even know when the mission was birthed in me. It was over 40 years ago when I met a woman who had such a profound impact on me that I felt compelled to find her twice in my adult life, once when I was in my mid 20's and again this past summer. She was a one-of-a-kind. She was genuine, loving, nurturing and she saw something very special in me. As far as I was concerned, no one else existed except for me. I was her student and she was my first grade teacher. Her name is Betty Clark. Mrs. Clark taught me how to read and write, but mostly she taught me that life isn't just about me. It's about others and making others feel special, unique and important. She was one of my early heroes and she made me want to do for others what she had done for me.

I'll never forget Mrs. Clark and the distinct dinner invitation she extended to me one evening. I was overjoyed to go to her house that night. I'm sure other kids would have killed for the opportunity, but she invited me and only me (as far as I know). We ate pork and beans and hot dogs, bread and butter and we had Kool Aid and cake for dessert. Wow, what a memory! You see, Mrs. Clark saw something in me that made her feel she needed to show me that I was valued and loved. It could not have come at a better time either because I had recently experienced a very difficult transition in my home life. My parents had recently divorced, I was living with my father and new stepmother at the start of first grade. And although I didn't quite have the language to express what I felt about the changes, somehow Mrs. Clark knew. She went above and beyond with me. She took me under her wings and showed me exactly what I needed at that moment in my life. She showed me love and attention and she made me want to emulate her. I wanted to be a teacher just like her. It became my childhood dream and aspiration.

I didn't know it yet, but what I really wanted out of life was to make a difference for others like she made a difference for me. I spent my life trying to make a difference in the lives of others and at some point in my life, I indeed became a teacher, just like Mrs. Clark. I believe I had a very positive impact on the lives of the students who crossed the threshold of my classroom doors and at some point, my dreams expanded because I wanted to impact a larger audience and make a difference on a broader scale and so I became a Principal.

Mrs. Clark was very proud of the adult I had become and even more proud that she had a part to play in it. Tears rolled down her cheeks as we talked this past summer and I was able to share how she influenced my life.

My dreams over the years changed and were influenced by various circumstances in my life, but all of them tied into my overarching life's purpose or theme.

Have you figured out what your purpose in life is yet? Years ago, Rick Warren wrote *The Purpose Driven Life*, purporting that all of us are here to live out the purpose of our creator, God. I don't know if you subscribe to this but I can certainly relate. Imagine you are the developer/creator of a technological device. You take great care to design the device with many intricacies, nuances, abilities and functions. You have a particular purpose for how the device will be used by mankind and so as you create it, you make sure that you include clues as to how the device is supposed to be used. You have knobs, buttons, switches and the like and all of the components of the device bring satisfaction to the user. Somehow it is made to make the life of the user more convenient. You know how it will help because you designed it that way. The device serves its purpose because when it is turned on, the user is able to enjoy it for the purpose in which it was created.

The same holds true for you. You've been created with certain gifts, talents, aptitude, intellect, abilities and skills. You may not know all that you possess at first, but the longer you live, the more you begin to get a glimpse into what all of those talents are used for and why you were created. You eventually realize the connection between who you are, what you do, what you like, what you are drawn to, driven by and what you'd like to do. You were born for some uniquely special reason. Your job is to find it through research, trial and error, and exploration, but the clues are there. Sometimes you need help, although there is no manual like with the electronic device in our previous example, but because you are still alive, there is still time to figure it out and begin to live it.

When I started searching, I discovered that my experiences all had a connection to who I am and why I was put here. Every dream I ever held for myself was connected to my overall purpose in life. I didn't always know it and I didn't always realize it, but when I look back over my life, it's as clear as day. What do you know about yourself? How do your experiences, dreams and choices connect? Can you see any patterns? This is not to say that you may not make mistakes and choose the wrong path from time to time, but how have those choices even impacted who you are and your overall purpose? What makes your heart sing, as one author poses the question? What makes you feel like you are in your blissful place? Or what do you imagine will make you feel most blissful? As in chapter one, what could or would you be doing if you could pick and not be judged or not fail or not need to make a living from it? What consumes your interest and time? These are all the clues into who you are and why you are on this earth. You can also ask your Creator. I know I did. I asked God to reveal to me why He put me on this earth. And He answered over and over again, showing me myself at different time periods and revealing exactly what I shared with you.

What is it that you dream about doing? Wish for when no one is watching? Or imagine for yourself, if only conditions were right? What do you long for in your wildest dreams? What on earth would you be doing if your dreams came true? It's okay if they've changed since a previous time you dared to dream. And it's okay if they don't seem feasible. Let me share another relevant story with you from my childhood.

"You will sing this song, whether you want to or not!" And the case was closed. I was 13 years old and I was being forced to participate in a special program at my church in which my youth director required that I sing an old song, "Impossible Dream". I didn't really have a choice in the matter. I was the pastor's kid and I pretty much had to do whatever I was told by the leaders. What made matters worse, this youth director was also one of my teachers in Jr. High school. I couldn't get away from her. Plus she had a reputation and you didn't want to get on her bad side. I dreaded being made to sing what I had determined was an old song, I was quite adamant about it, even going so far as to sass my youth director and storm out of the room. My teenage boldness was in rare form as I tried to argue my case and stand my ground, but in the end, I lost the battle. I was still required to sing the song, which I grudgingly did. As it turned out, I actually did a pretty good job with the song and I don't think the audience ever knew the fight I had and lost.

Like most teens, I couldn't appreciate the rich lyrics of this moving song. Truthfully, I didn't really want to. I stood there, pouting, with my lips poked out, sullen, waiting for the last phrase so I could sit down. Thank God for adulthood and maturity. If I only knew then the significance of these lyrics and their ties to my message today, I could have saved myself the heartache. Take a look at the last stanza of the song:

*To reach the unreachable,*
*the unreachable,*
*The unreachable star*
*And I'll always dream*
*The impossible dream*
*Yes, and I'll reach*
*The unreachable star*

It is a song that talks about reaching the unreachable star and dreaming the impossible dream...very moving. The song was a song of hope and encouragement. It's been sung by many famous artists. The message of the song brings to mind the importance of dreaming dreams, not the ones we have when we're sleeping, but the ones we have when we're awake. It's when we conceive those dreams that we are taking a step in acquiring a life of fulfillment and satisfaction. It's those dreams that every successful person points to and credits for the beginning of their successes. Your dreams could do the same for you, but you have to be able to identify them and claim them.

Eleanor Roosevelt once said, *"The future belongs to those who believe in the beauty of their dreams."* Think about that statement in the context of famous, successful people like Bill Gates, Michael Jordan, or any other successful person you may know. Think about it in the context of you. You can even substitute your own name in the quote, like this: *The future belongs to _____ (insert your name), who believes in the beauty of my dreams.* How does that sound to you? Your dream may seem impossible, like Bill Gates who dreamed of creating personal computers for people to use at home. Let's face it, at that time, personal computers were not even a thing yet. He dreamed an impossible dream, then went to work to make it a reality. He believed in the beauty of his dreams. Belief is a big part of fulfillment. We'll talk about that more in detail in the next chapter.

This concept of believing in the beauty of your dreams is what I want to talk about in this chapter, it's **the first principle** towards making success happen in your life. **The principle**

**is to Dream**. I define a dream as the vision, aspiration or ambition you imagine for yourself personally and/or professionally. These dreams are usually connected to your overall purpose and mission in life, the reason why you are here on this earth. And one of the overarching messages I want you to walk away with is that your dreams matter.

Let's talk about this all too familiar concept of dreaming. Dreaming is critical if you are going to live a life of fulfillment. It gives us a look inside at our purpose. Everyone has dreams, although you may not acknowledge or give credence to them. I also believe God gives us dreams, which are hard to ignore because they don't usually go away. Truthfully, not all dreams are significant and meant to be pursued. But those "God-dreams" are quite important because they are usually bigger than you and will have a major impact on others. They are definitely tied to your purpose. And it makes sense too, because those dreams answer questions you have about your life. Your dreams can change the world that we live in and the people that you interact with in life. To dream, even those impossible dreams, can change your very circumstances and others for the better.

I do want to warn you that dreaming alone will not lead to a life of fulfillment. Dreaming is just an early step on the fulfillment road. Dreaming is hopeful and can leave you in a euphoric state. Dreaming is not reality just yet. Dreaming doesn't work out all of the kinks and dreaming is certainly not a plan of action. Dreaming is the beginning. It allows you to imagine and see into your future, but it is not your future. I think that's why dreamers get a bad reputation, because they stop at the dreaming phase and do not go any further. All they ever talk about are their dreams, hopes and wishes, but do not take any steps to make them reality. Dreaming needs to lead to action and action to fulfillment. If you remain in a dream state, you sound irrational and may make impulsive moves without considering the costs. You then risk being viewed by those close to you as a nutcase and you lose credibility for your next great idea. If you lose credibility, you are in danger of losing support from those you need to support you.

I love a great dream and I am capable of dreaming for days and coming up with hundreds of creative ideas and solutions to different problems, but if none of my dreams are connected to my purpose and followed up with meaningful action, they are all for naught. Dreaming to no end is a waste of time, in my opinion. It's like brainstorming without following up with narrowing your ideas and using those ideas to make a decision. Let me also draw a distinction between brainstorming and dreaming. A brainstorm allows you the freedom to think of as many ideas as you can without consequence or judgment. But a brainstorm doesn't equate to a dream. The decision to expand upon a brainstorming session is important so that you narrow your ideas to ones that can realistically be developed, possibly into a dream. Dreams can be birthed from brainstorming sessions, circumstances that happen in your life or from God, but again, must be followed up with some action. We'll develop this thought further as we go through this book. When it comes to brainstorming vs. dreaming, I can speak from personal experience. I've spent many days in my lifetime dreaming of what could be and not doing anything more with those dreams and ideas than just drumming them up in my head. Eventually, they fall to the wayside. However, the significant dreams, those God-given dreams will outlast all the others and when they are combined with my other 5 principles can lead to something awesome.

Remember in the previous chapter I mentioned having started a nonprofit organization while I was in my 20's? Let me tell you a little more about that. It was a total uphill climb for me, but such a valuable learning experience. I can never forget those early days. I was employed by another non-profit in a program that helped those who had never completed high school prepare for their GED and learn foundational skills in math and reading. I was the director of the program and I had a few staff members reporting to me. The organization was a well-established organization in the community and had a long standing reputation for the various social services that they offered to the community. They also had a couple of day care centers that they operated, where I had my own young child during the day.

It didn't take long for me to become frustrated with the organization each pay day when it became a race to the bank to see who could cash their paychecks first. Can you imagine that? You've worked hard for a pay period only to find out that you may not be able to cash your paycheck. This happened nearly every payday. Sometimes the paycheck would just bounce. I don't know about you, but for me I couldn't continue to work for an organization whose integrity was in question. What's more, the bosses never communicated to the staff that they were having problems meeting payroll.

Let me pause for a moment to give you a glimpse inside. Notice my frustration was centered around the organization's lack of character and integrity. Integrity and character are values that I hold dear. It is very inconsistent to me that you can be an organization that "helps" people and not live up to a basic characteristic called integrity. Their lack of integrity "hurt" more people than the organization was helping. Knowing what you value, what you deem as important will also help you in figuring out your purpose.

Out of sheer frustration and an entrepreneurial spirit, I tendered my resignation from the company and started my own nonprofit organization. I don't even recall exactly when the dream was birthed, but I believe circumstances led me to dream of starting my own organization, where we could help people and not hurt others in the process. I also knew that I could not continue to work in a place that had such uncertainty. I sat down with my husband and a few other supportive individuals and I dreamed of the type of organization I would build. As you might imagine, it was absolutely in line with my purpose of making a difference, I just hadn't reflected on my life long enough to know it yet.

I did the research on how to start a nonprofit, filled out the necessary paperwork, including the grueling 501c3 and submitted it for approval to the IRS. My dream was to build an organization that worked with socio-economically disadvantaged individuals providing educational and artistic programming. It allowed me to combine my interest in education and the arts. I named it after my grandfather, who was a huge proponent for education and the arts. It was a befitting honor to bestow upon him. He had gone through a lot in his life and didn't earn his GED until he was a senior citizen. However, he believed in all of his children and grandchildren getting a good education. He was very gifted as an artist, painting dozens, if not hundreds of paintings in his day; he was also a writer, a musical composer, a choir director and he played the piano. My dream allowed me to honor him and make a difference for some deserving individuals.

Unfortunately, I was so limited in my knowledge of running

and operating a nonprofit organization, that I was not able to raise adequate funds to sustain programming. Eventually, I had to close down the organization, but not before learning a host of lessons. Not all dreams will survive at first, especially if they are devoid of the proper support and resources. Remember, dreaming is only the beginning of making things happen in your life that will lead to fulfillment.

Fortunately, I was not discouraged with the failure of the nonprofit. I was simply fueled to dream bigger later down the road. Just because a dream doesn't turn out as planned doesn't mean that you stop dreaming. Sometimes the failure of a dream is meant to be so that you can grow as an individual. I am a fan of seeing the lessons life has to offer as a gift. This failure taught me many lessons about life and helped me with future endeavors. So your lesson here is to keep dreaming and keep learning even if the dream seems to end up being a dead end.

So what is it about dreaming that is so powerful? Dreams open the door to your purpose or passion. Without dreams, purpose is not fully realized. Without dreams, we can simply just go through the motions of life doing what's predictable or doing what others require of us or doing what we're good at doing and never following the path that leads to our destiny or purpose. Countless people choose to do what they're good at, but are never fulfilled or even happy. Recently I had a conversation with a woman who told me those very words. She is an entrepreneur who owns a successful business in the fashion industry. But you wouldn't believe what she was doing before she had her own business. She shared with me in a phone conversation that she had a degree in Accounting and was working as an accountant, earning a great salary. She was very good at her accounting job, but woke up one day and realized that she didn't feel gratification as an accountant although she was considered successful. Financial success also doesn't equate to life fulfillment. This fashion designer/entrepreneur went through her own self-discovery and decided to dream. In doing so, she was able to tap into something that she always loved doing. She loved to shop and she took great joy from styling other individuals who would come to her for direction in fashion. She said to me, "I was very good at being an accountant, but I didn't love it." So she set out to change her circumstances. Today she enjoys wonderful success as a fashion designer, editor of a fashion magazine and speaker. Dreams have the ability to change your path and ultimately change your life. Anything I've ever done personally or professionally started with a dream.

So why is dreaming often overlooked or minimized by so many? Why do people undervalue dreams? Could it be because they don't realize how purpose is fulfilled through dreams? Let me further illustrate. Remember in the previous chapter I told you about my business venture of becoming an

Independent Beauty Consultant? Had I not stepped out and ambitiously pursued the business, I would not be able to do what I do today. When I joined the company and started working for myself as a beauty consultant, I unlocked something within, while overcoming a major fear of public speaking. You see, once I started working the business, I quickly realized I could reach higher levels in the business and gain some desirable perks, including driving a free car! That incentive appealed to me. I did what was required of me in record time and became a Director, earned my car and a unit of ladies I had to lead and support weekly. I also had to provide training to the unit weekly.

When I became a director, I was petrified to speak in front of people and this role was requiring that I do it every single week. Sure, I stood in front of children as their teacher, but this was different. Children didn't judge me like adults had the potential to do. So this was a big deal for me. Sometimes you'll have to face and overcome some major fears on your journey to finding purpose and fulfillment. I'll never forget the first time I had to introduce myself to an audience of women at one of the weekly meetings (prior to becoming a director). My stomach was in knots! I was passing gas uncontrollably. I know this sounds funny, but my fear of speaking in front of groups was very real, but I forced myself to do it. My dream of becoming a director was far greater than my fear, so I fought through my fear and stepped up to the microphone, cleared my throat and introduced myself. I would have to do this numerous times before I became a director and was given the responsibility to not just introduce myself, but conduct those weekly training sessions. I had to step into a role that I had never really experienced previously. The miracle of this experience was how it prepared me for my current life as a trainer, speaker and business owner. I now speak for a living and get paid to do it! Had I not pursued the temporal dream of being a director, I would not be able to do what I do now.

*******************************

Unfortunately, not everyone is comfortable admitting they have dreams and/or sharing their dreams. And sadly, not everyone dares to dream. Why is this so? My guess is because dreams are not always supported and respected by those with whom dreams are shared. Let's face it, not everyone will respect your dreams. Not everyone respects my dreams. And when others have expectations of you and have decided that you should be doing certain things, they put you in a box and do not give you permission to come out of the box and try new things. If you shared your "out of the box" dreams with those who have you in a box, you will be met with dissatisfaction, laughter, rejection, and possibly anger and disappointment.

These naysayers may not value the significance of your dreams, may not believe that you should follow a dream or they simply are not supportive.  Perhaps they just don't know to value your dreams.  I can understand why you might be apprehensive to share your dreams and quite honestly, I would recommend that you keep them to yourself until you've had time to internalize them and feel secure and safe enough to share.  I believe in protecting your dreams so that at the appropriate time they can be nurtured and cultivated.

Dreams also need to be visualized.  They gain traction when you can see yourself doing something new and different.  If you actually pictured what it would be like to walk in your dreams, interact with people as you are living your dreams and how your dreams would affect your life, you give your dreams worth.  As I was first drafting this chapter on dreams, I shared my draft with my husband and his response was a little unexpected.  He said, he had never given any thought to how dreams can be so significant.  I responded to him, "How could you not?  It's what you did over 25 years ago when you dreamed of your future career.  Remember how your aunt used to tell you to, 'Put it on the screen?'"  He chuckled because I jogged his memory of conversations he would often have with his now 90 year old aunt when he was a young professional.  She would tell him to visualize what he wanted to achieve.  Her way of describing the visualization or dreaming process was to "Put it on the screen".  That was her way of encouraging him to picture himself doing what he wanted to accomplish in his future.  She is a wise woman.  The amazing thing about this visualization exercise was that all these years later, he accomplished exactly what he "Put on the screen". He often looked at his screen to remind him of his dream.

Engaging in this conversation with him was amusing to me because it was a perfect example of how people don't realize the power of their dreams. He "put it on the screen" that he wanted to be a superior court judge and sure enough, he achieved exactly what he dreamed. It didn't come without the other principles that we'll discuss in this book, but it started as a dream on the screen of his mind. He never lost sight of his dream and he was safe to share it with me and even his aunt because we both understood the power of that mental picture. If he had kept his dream to himself all of those years, he may never have had the opportunity and support to pursue it. What do you have on your screen? And who do you have in your corner to share it with? Find someone safe, who will support you.

I'm troubled when I hear stories of dreams deferred, ignored, disrespected or disregarded, because like Eleanor Roosevelt, I believe in the beauty of dreams. I've seen firsthand how a powerful dream has changed lives. When dreams are shunned, rather than celebrated and pursued, futures are altered. A colleague of mine recently recommended I read a book called, **Die Empty** by Todd Henry. I downloaded the audio version of the book to listen to it. Henry talks about a similar theme, one of living a fulfilling life. He shares stories and steps for how it's done. Essentially, Henry wants us to consider living a life of no regrets. Who wants to go to their graves regretting not living the life of their dreams? No one knows when their life will end, but wouldn't it be nicer if we all lived it to the fullest?

I cannot tell you the countless times I've heard people disregard and even discredit another's dreams, arguing that they are lofty and unrealistic. This air of discouragement is often the reason people won't take the time to pursue their dreams and therefore give up on them. Dreams are meant to be pursued, especially when they are tied to your destiny. Find a way to keep your dreams alive and protected.

Destiny filled dreams should not remain in their dream state just because they seem unattainable or difficult to visualize or get support. I would encourage you to hold fast to the dreams that are worth pursuing because they can change the trajectory of your and others' lives. Unfortunately, many people will die with unfulfilled dreams inside of them and the world will essentially be deprived of what could have been. How sad.

It's tough to have a dream or vision of something new and special and not live it or pursue it, but I get it. Dreams can be risky, scary and unpredictable. These may be reason enough for most people not to want to be considered "a dreamer" as dreamers get a bad rap. When identified as a dreamer, others may view you as one of those "head in the clouds" types I referenced earlier and not take you seriously. That's unfortunate, but a very real possibility. I believe dreams are important. My daughter recently shared a fortune from inside her fortune cookie and the subject could not have been more appropriate. It read, *"A man's dreams are an index to his greatness."* It's exactly what I'm saying here. One doesn't become great without having a dream and then taking a risk to follow that dream.

When my husband "Put it on the screen," he visualized it and kept it at the forefront of his mind for more than 2 decades! Whenever he needed to remind himself of where he was going, he could simply look up at his imaginary screen and see his dream or life accomplishment before him. This sometimes is all he needed to keep pursuing. His aunt understood the importance and value of a dream and its connection to one's destiny. She understood that he needed to dream it, see it, and then pursue it. That's exactly what he did, but he took it a step further. He talked about it. He told me in our first year of marriage what his ultimate professional dream was and he was more than a decade away from it even being a possibility. At that early stage, he was a very inexperienced professional and needed a minimum of 10 years practicing law before he could attain his dream and even then, it would     take persistence and patience. Though he had to wait to actively pursue his dream due to the nature of the circumstances, he did not let time stop him from keeping it in the forefront of his mind and bringing it up in conversation at various points along his journey.

He would not have been able to talk about his dream if he didn't have a safe place to discuss it. He had to know that I as the listener was going to hear him, support him and not dismiss or ignore him. As a dreamer, you need a safe environment in order to be comfortable enough to share your dreams with others. If you do not have a supportive listener, you may find you have to bury or hide your dream or you may choose to defer it rather than pursue it. This is precisely why you have to be very careful who you share your dreams with because people can take your dreams and stomp all over them, leaving you feeling down and devoid of courage. Dreaming takes courage.

I also believe dreams need to be protected until you're confident that the listener of your dreams will provide support without judgment. When I wanted to pursue the dream of starting my educational consulting firm, I needed to approach it carefully because it involved one of the biggest risks I had ever taken in my life. I didn't just spring it on people, I nursed it a while, let it evolve, wrote it down and researched the possibilities of it. That was how I protected and nurtured my dream until the timing was right to share it with the parties that it affected.

Think of the many successful individuals, famous or not so famous that you can imagine. All of them attained success because they once conceived a dream in their minds. What we can't easily see is how their dreams were nurtured and cultivated. But I can assure you that every dream has to take different forms before it becomes reality. Dreams in their raw state are just that. They need to be nurtured by you before you can expect to see them come to life.

Let's take one of my mentees who had a dream to go to college one day, in particular a certain top 100 university in the country. The dream was birthed at the least likely time of her life. She was a middle school drop-out at the time, having suffered from abuse, depression and suicidal thoughts. She was the daughter of a mother dealing with serious issues (which she eventually overcame) and she was probably the last person you'd imagine in a college setting. She was very rough around the edges, had a lot of anger and struggled tremendously for someone who was only 13 years old. But she had a dream.

Her dream was inspired by my sharing my college experience with her and feeding her hope that she too could go to college. There were no other individuals in her life at the time who had the ability to encourage her and so she had to nurture her dream on her own. She started one step at a time. Her first step was to get a GED which was difficult at first because she was a poor math student. Eventually, she succeeded, then she enrolled in the local two year college and struggled her way to earning her Associates Degree. She never lost sight of her dream to go to a four year college. She even applied to her coveted university and was accepted, but couldn't afford to attend, so she chose to attend a well-regarded state university.

Initially, it took her a while to matriculate through her Associates Program and then transfer to a four year college where she earned her first Bachelor's degree. She has since earned additional degrees and is studying for her MCAT to go to medical school. Since earning her degrees, she's been fortunate to land a lucrative job at a pharmaceutical company in clinical research. She's married and is doing very well in her life and has many other dreams to fulfill, but it all started with an unlikely, perhaps impossible dream. She nurtured her dream by working through each step of it and never giving up when the going got tough, which it did.

There were distractions and challenges along the way, but she never lost sight of the bigger dream to earn her college degree and so she worked at each level, taking all the necessary steps to reach her goals and realize her dreams. She nurtured her dreams much like we parents nurture our children. We take care of them. She took care of her dreams, she kept them alive within her mind and continued to feed her dreams by working one class at a time to earn her degree. As with children, we encourage them to grow and she did the same thing with her dream, she didn't stop at one degree, she continued to pursue all the way to present day where she is waiting to go to medical school. She never stopped learning along the way, another way to nurture your dreams. You must continue to learn what you can to take you to the next level.

When I first started my career as a principal, I was coming on board to turn the school around. The school had not been doing very well in terms of student achievement in academics. The demographics were viewed by some as challenging. There was a high transient rate, students moved a lot from one community to another and many did not stay in the same school for more than a year, let alone for the span of their elementary years. Teachers were very dedicated, but their morale was low because students struggled to pass the state assessment year after year, leaving the school with a label of being a school in need of improvement. This label was given by the state department of education. It was not an honor. It carried a huge stigma in the community and we were seen by some as the black sheep in the district.

There are many schools like this school, with similar demographics of students from lower socio-economic backgrounds, many of whom lived with one parent and they struggled to master literacy skills at the point they were expected to master them. When I started at the school, I immediately fell in love with the students and found them to be very bright with hopeful futures. I believed they could be successful and I then set out to dream what some might have thought was an impossible dream. I dreamed they could see and know success. I was able to envision them thriving in school and learning and growing academically.

I dreamed that the school would be removed from the state's lists of schools in need of improvement and we were going to Make it Happen. That dream is what others would call a vision. When you are leading an organization, you must first develop a vision of what the organization could become or accomplish. Any good leader must start with a vision of what could be in the days, months and even years to come. I had a vision that my students would be able to grow and show growth for at least two years in a row to remove them from the state's list. I knew that they could do it (I believed it) and I made sure that my entire team not only became familiar with my vision, but adopted it as theirs as well. I had to clearly articulate what my dream was for the school and then provide my team with the support and resources they needed to Make it Happen. My vision was to get students excited about reading and writing so that they could begin to demonstrate growth. But ultimately, their being able to read and write would give them success in life, not just school.

I took my dream for the school and students very seriously. My vision is what drove my decision making. My vision was tied to the destiny of the school. This dream was destined to become reality because students' lives depended upon it. Their success was more than just a notion to me. I was determined to make it a reality. My dream was followed up with numerous mini-dreams. For example, we needed students to become excited about reading and writing, so we had to make reading and writing fun. We had to brainstorm ideas of how to make it exciting and then go to work to make it a reality.

Some of those ideas that became a reality was for me to start a before school reading club, which I volunteered to run, manage various independent reading challenges with desirable incentives, schedule book exchanges among students, pay for reader's theater after school programming, and many more. I even wrote and published a children's chapter book for younger students. The bigger picture dream of getting students excited about reading and writing grew legs and eventually led to improved results in reading/writing performance. Never underestimate the power of a dream/vision. There is a scripture that states, without a vision, the people perish. *(Proverbs 29:18)* Had I not had the dream to improve reading/writing, students' literacy skills may not have grown as much as they did.

Another example of when I had a dream was related to my dream of becoming a school principal. I envisioned it relatively early in my teaching career that administration would be my next move, and I set out to Make it Happen. I first went back to school online to earn my Master's Degree. That was quite a feat. It took me longer than I had expected because I had to stop taking classes during the time that I was recovering from that pivotal car accident.

My dream, like any of yours, started with a notion, perhaps a calling of sorts. I knew this was going to be a part of my journey. I had to nurture the dream, which entailed finding a preparation program that could complement my busy lifestyle. In other words, if you want something, you'll find a way to Make it Happen. I was working full time, as a teacher, taking two classes every eight weeks, while playing the role of football/basketball/dance mom, running my kids back and forth to their extra-curricular activities multiple times a week and I was a wife.

Pursuing your dreams may not be easy. You may have to jump through some hoops, crowd your schedule, live life a little unbalanced for a while, and go through challenges, like I did, but in the end, it's worth it. I admire busy people, because busy people get things done! Busy people will make temporary sacrifices for long term gain.

Those years while I was finishing my Master's program were

demanding and even entailed a few tears as I stayed up night after night praying I would be able to hit the "submit" button before the midnight deadline. But I did it! Sure there were interruptions to my plans. Interruptions are bound to happen. Don't let interruptions become permanent and keep you from your destiny. Interruptions and distractions are a part of the territory and can come along at inopportune times, but recognize them and work around them.

This was still the first step to fulfilling my dream of becoming a principal. Eventually, I finished my program, which included an internship with my boss (the school's principal) and graduated with a 4.0! Step 1, down! Next I had to pass the national exam. That was also very hard. The studying process was intense and the impending exam promised to be one of the hardest I'd ever had to date. I always panicked when it came to standardized tests. I always felt like I didn't test well, so I had a lot of anxiety. This negative mindset was a waste of energy. I learned that lesson later. The exam was over 6 hours long and the day of the exam it was very hot outside (I hate the heat) and the test was in a building that had no air conditioning. Not good! And the exam was all essay! I couldn't guess my way through the exam. I had to know what I was doing and I had to sound good doing it. I'll never forget how anxious I was that day. I was never able to relax!

When I left the exam and finally got into my air conditioned car, I broke down crying! The whole day's experience was beyond intense. It was arduous and stressful. But don't miss the point. I didn't avoid the challenge, I faced it because I had goals and dreams to nurture. I pushed through the challenge. I fought through it. Fighting is a concept that a lot of people avoid, but I want to help you tap into your fight when the issue is worth fighting for.

Believe me, it's not always easy fulfilling a dream, but like I said before, it's worth it! I wouldn't want to do it again but I would. And besides, when I look on the bright side, as it turned out, I did exceptionally well on that exam earning 191 out of a possible 200 points.

Pursuing your dreams can definitely be tough, but there are rewards too. Those rewards remind you that the journey is worth it! Life is a journey. Pursuing your dreams is a journey. If we didn't go through challenges on the journey, we probably would take the journey for granted and our growth would be limited. Challenges build character. Plus the journeys with tests and trials are the journeys that make good stories to tell in the end.

As a young girl, I often heard elderly people talking about life and the negative encounters we may experience and remarking there can't be a testimony without a test. And that's the beauty of pursuing your dreams. The journey may discourage you and make you want to give it up, but keep going. Anything worth having, is worth the pursuit.

At this point of my journey, I still had not attained my goal of becoming a principal. I was at the part of the journey where I had to apply to the state for certification and then pursue administrative opportunities. Sometimes pursuing your dreams take time before you see it come to fruition, but you must stay the course and keep pushing.

## Tonya's Take Aways

*"The future belongs to those who believe in the beauty of their dreams." (Eleanor Roosevelt)* **Dreaming is an important process in our lives as it gives us a window into our purpose and drives us towards living a fulfilling life. When you have a dream that is meant to be pursued, you need to "Put it on the Screen", visualize it, and see it as your vision. Remember that your vision must be nurtured by taking the steps needed to "Make it Happen". Don't get discouraged when obstacles and barriers come along to interrupt or distract you away from your dreams. That's a part of life and even expected on some level. Push through your challenges and fight to Make it Happen in your life, business or career.**

# 4 HAVE FAITH

"You can't be a principal without serving in the capacity of Vice Principal for several years." That was a statement that was spoken to me by a school administrator early in my career. I had not yet been a school administrator, but was looking forward to the opportunity. You should know that I highly respected the professionals in my industry, in particular school leaders and this was one of those with whom I had a lot of respect, but that comment did not resonate positively at all within me. All I heard was "YOU CAN'T..." I didn't need to hear anything else. I could feel heat rising within as disdain for the comment filled my body. I had to control my boiling blood and resist the urge to lash out, *"You obviously do not know me!"* I succeeded and kept my mouth shut. I kept my composure and simply nodded as though I agreed with the statement. But I did not agree at all. In fact, I almost saw it as a dare or at least as a challenge. I have never taken words of doubt too kindly from anyone and this time was no different. What this administrator didn't know about me was that when I set my mind to doing something and combine it with the belief that I can do something, I usually do just that. I told you already, I make things happen! And this time was no different.

Essentially, anyone who ever expresses doubt about what I can accomplish will be proven wrong, EVENTUALLY. That's because my belief system is far stronger than their projections of doubt. Hearing the statement that I could not become a school principal early in my administrative career was one such statement! Although it was well meaning coming from the speaker, it rang very negatively in my ears. It was all I needed to hear to propel me into pursuing my next dream in life.

I started the next school year as a teacher in an out-of-classroom assignment, but by the 2nd marking period/quarter of the school year, I was an Interim Vice Principal. That role lasted the remainder of the school year and then I was off to my next assignment. Can you guess what it was? You've guessed right if you guessed that I was a principal next, not a Vice Principal. In fact, my role as a vice principal was less than one year. My husband likes to jokingly say to me, "You don't play around." That's his way of acknowledging that when I put my mind to something, I Make it Happen. Once I took the unwitting dare to become a principal, I became a principal.

I really want you to hone in on the power of the mind because this is the key to you being able to make things happen for yourself. The **2nd Principle is to HAVE FAITH.** Faith is all about your belief and beliefs are from the mind. Your mind, thoughts, and beliefs are strong contributors to whether you can accomplish something. In other words, your faith determines what you can accomplish. Let's look deeper into the impact faith and beliefs have on your life, career or business.

My beliefs have gotten me very far in life. Another example of it was when I was a high school senior, and wanted to attend only one university in this country, Howard University, a very prestigious HBCU (Historically Black College/University). Howard usually ranks as one of the top 100 schools in the nation and I knew from the time I was a freshman in high school and heard about it from a fellow high school alumnae, that this was the school for me. The alum was named Robin. Robin was a ball of energy and excitement. He was three years my senior and he was a very popular leader I was proud to know even as a freshman in high school. After graduating and attending Howard for the first year, Robin returned to our high school and talked to a group of us about his experience at "the Mecca" as it was affectionately called and he shared stories about his phenomenal experience as a student and what Howard had to offer students. I made up my mind right then and there that I was going to Howard University, sight unseen.

As you might guess, when it was time for me to apply, I only applied there, no place else. The naysayers would say, "Don't put all your eggs in one basket," and of course I ignored them all. Even at that tender age I believed and knew that I would not only get accepted, but I would attend there in the fall after graduation. Plus, I worked hard as a student. My scholarly pursuits were very serious to me. It had been ingrained in me as a young girl...education was going to be the key to getting anything I wanted out of life. I knew that I would attend the school of my dreams. Nothing would stand in my way and nothing would stop me from going...nothing.

-----------------------------------------------------------------

Success was in the air that spring afternoon when my mom told me I had a letter from Howard University. I knew what it was the moment I saw the envelope. It was thick and it had a lot of papers inside. My heart thumped so hard it could have been possible for my mother to see it beating through my shirt. I tore into the envelope and all I needed to see was the word, "Congratulations..." I don't remember any other words. I leaped for joy because the life that I believed for myself would soon be happening to me. Whoo hoo! My dream was coming true. I love the mind and the power it wields!

-----------------------------------------------------------------

When it was time for me to go away to college, my parents also had to take my brother to college, to a smaller HBCU in

Virginia. He and I were both going away for the first time and we had never been apart. We started first grade together and we were always together. We walked to school together from the time we were in elementary school until high school. We were very close. In middle and high school, we were always in the same homeroom and other classes as well. We also ran track together. I'm sure the thought of us separating and me being in the big city of Washington, DC made my parents a little nervous, perhaps downright scared. But I was excited, as many young college freshmen are at the start of their new school year.

I'll never forget that August after my senior year in high school, motor home all packed up with my brother's and my college doodads and we were all set to get on the road. The first stop was Richmond, Virginia where my brother would be attending school. He had to be there one full week ahead of me. In those days my father drove a motor home or recreational vehicle that slept 5-6 people and we were using that to move us into our new temporary homes on our respective college campuses. The ride was rather leisurely and enjoyable as we were both starting new journeys into adulthood. Finally we arrived at his campus, moved him into his tiny dormitory room and did all the things families do when they take their children to college for the first time. It was a quaint campus and the people were very friendly. Southern hospitality permeated the campus and the nurturing environment seemed to make a strong impression on my parents.

We were standing on the campus in front of my brother's dorm when my mother tried to convince me to transfer to my brother's school because it was smaller and people would know my name. *Is she crazy?!?! I'm not going here, I'm going to Howard!!!*    She even went so far as to say the following statement, which obviously had a negative impact on me.  She said, "You could be a queen at this small college, you'll never be a queen at Howard." Her words screeched like fingernails scratching the chalkboard.    They were quite unwelcomed and I refused to listen to them because they were very contrary to my dreams.  She was not necessarily being literal with the queen reference, but I only heard that I can't be/do something.  The reasoning was not relevant for me at the time.  I heard her silently, unknowingly challenging me, daring me even to be a queen on Howard's campus.  She thought she was simply trying to make a point that this smaller, hospitable campus could be a great place for me and I wouldn't get lost in the numbers. She was well meaning in her thoughts, but I received it differently.  To me, I was provoked to prove that I could be more than just a number of the much larger Howard University.  I could and would be a queen!

The mind and its beliefs are very powerful.  As you might have guessed, I did become a queen at Howard. I was Miss Liberal Arts and represented the School of Liberal Arts in the campus wide pageant. The pageant was so far outside of anything I had ever done in my life, but it was something I had to prove and I was determined to make my point. I was a junior by that time and when I heard about the pageant, I inquired. I even put my life on hold to prepare for it, which turned out not to be a good choice. After winning at the school of Liberal Arts, I moved on to the university pageant. The winner of the larger pageant would be Miss Howard University, would get her name and photo in the acclaimed Ebony Magazine and would also be known throughout the campus and community. I confess, I was intimidated by the process, but I was committed to it because I had set my mind to it. I was competing against the queens from the other campus schools, Fine Arts, Business, Education, Social Work, Nursing, Allied Health, etc. Although I didn't win the larger pageant, I did win Miss Congeniality. My prize for winning at my school level was a trip for two to the Bahamas, so I wasn't terribly disappointed. The point here that I really want to drive home is the importance of having the ambition and belief to accomplish anything in life. For me, one was to become a principal and another a queen. In each instance, my belief and faith were the strongest contributors to making them a reality.

I said it in the introductory chapter, what our minds can conceive can indeed be achieved. Think about what people have been able to accomplish by simply conceiving it in their minds. Recently, I watched a movie about the late Steve Jobs, the acclaimed computer guru who was behind the success of Apple, Inc. When you look at what that technology company was able to create for the benefit of its consumers, what you see is nothing short of amazing. These devices that we often take for granted are very precise machines that can perform complex tasks that make our lives easier. Every single device created by Apple, Inc. was conceived in the minds of some very talented individuals. My first degree is in Psychology, where I studied the brain and behavior. I was always fascinated by the brain and its capabilities as it related to our behaviors. Our brains or minds are capable of performing significantly more than we ever use of it. Meaning, we only use a small percentage of our brains on a regular basis. If we chose to use more of our brain to accomplish new exploits in life, we could...although it may be challenging. Essentially, if you conceive an idea that you want to pursue, you are designed to be able to do it. You may need resources to help you, but you can pretty much do anything you choose to do, if you believe it. That's what's so remarkable about our human brain. So when I make the statement that we can achieve what we conceive, it's not just because I have been able to accomplish a lot in the span of my life, but it's because I strongly believe and have faith that my brain is capable of doing anything and there is a lot of evidence to support it. All we have to do is look around at what mankind has been able to produce.

The mindset is often overlooked in situations when you are looking to get ahead in life, your career or business. It dictates whether you will be successful and accomplish your dreams. The mindset is what motivates you to move forward with your plans or it can be what hinders you from moving forward. Your mindset comprises the decisions you make about yourself, your identity, your role, your goals and essentially all of the components that make you who you are and what you are capable of doing. For example, think about someone you know who is very ambitious. What do you notice about him or her? They seem to be driven towards many endeavors, whether all the ducks are lined up in a row or not. They are the people who defy odds and accomplish greatness. They are energized and give off vibes of success, even in the face of failure.

Conversely, think about someone you know who has very low ambition. They tend to lack motivation to do much more than the status quo, whatever that is. They procrastinate, they lean more towards a mundane existence, exhibit low energy and drive. They may be very talented and gifted, but something is stopping them from reaching new heights of excellence or success. The difference between the two could very well be locked inside of them in the form of their mindset. If you were to question both about their futures, one may demonstrate greater enthusiasm and optimism, while the other may take a more hum drum approach and give you excuses for why they can't or won't do anything more with their lives, careers or businesses.

The mind can help you overcome nearly all obstacles placed in your way on your journey towards becoming the best and most successful you. Sometimes the mindset is as simple as you making a decision. Recently, I was diagnosed with the Shingles virus. I didn't know I had it for over a week, although I was having symptoms. When I finally figured I should go to the doctor, suspecting that I had Shingles, I made up in my mind and declared emphatically that, "I may have Shingles, BUT Shingles will not have me!" I made up in my mind that I didn't have time for Shingles and I was not going to give in to the pain or discomfort it is widely known for causing in patients. In one week's time following the doctor's visit, I was totally Shingles free. People, including the doctor, were amazed. I wasn't. I expected it to go away and leave me alone. I never gave in mentally to the condition and all of its negativity. I had too much to do and I didn't have time to be down. Have you ever heard the statement, "mind over matter"? Well I believe this was an example of it. My mind was more powerful than my diagnosis. Essentially, I had faith and believed that I would not be stopped by my ailment.

What if you began to train your mind to overpower negative thoughts that hinder you in any way? What if you began to take captive every negative thought that entered your mind? To do this, you must be willing to completely examine your thoughts about anything. You must challenge every ounce of negativity and make a decision to rid your mind of it and replace it with something more positive. You have to be willing to be honest and transparent, even with yourself first before you can even begin to tackle this. You may also need an accountability partner to point out to you when you are drifting into negative mind space. Don't be afraid to ask yourself some hard questions about what you think about yourself, where you are in your life in terms of your ambitions, what are your real thoughts about doing something different or new?

The next time someone asks you about what's next in your life, career or business, pause. Don't respond right away. Give yourself time to sift through your response and test it. What would a believing person think and say? Would their words be full of doubt, insecurity and negativity? Or will they boast of confidence, assurance and positivity? Will you speak as though you expect to reach your new goals? Will you even be able to speak to new goals set for your future? Because if you are stagnant in your life, career or business, can you grow? People who make things happen in their lives are always thinking of ways to continue developing personally and they are always looking for opportunities to learn and grow.

The difference between someone who has a positive versus negative mindset can be found in their language, in the words that they speak. When people are having conversations, listen to how they frame their circumstances, what perspective are they giving you? Are they talking about a challenge in a way that you walk away knowing they will overcome it or will the challenge overcome them? Everyone faces challenges, it's how we choose to see them that dictates how we handle them. The person with the greatest level of faith and most positive mindset will tackle the challenge almost as though it weren't challenging. They tend to maintain a positive, yet focused mindset about addressing the challenge. They have a certain resolve about them, a resolve that lets you know that they will conquer this challenge and live to tell a story about it.

What about you? How do you typically view and address challenges in your life? When was your last challenge and how did you see it?

I experienced a major challenge the year I became Miss Liberal Arts. I made a passing reference to it earlier. While going through the process of becoming a queen, I made a major sacrifice. I lost focus on the real reason for my being in school and my grades suffered like never before. My GPA that semester dropped significantly and I was mortified! In an effort to prove that I could do and become anything I set my mind to, I simultaneously took my mind off of my studies and paid for it with my formerly impressive GPA. Unfortunately, I only had 3 semesters remaining and I had to put my faith into play again to turn it around and bring my GPA back up before graduation. I could have stayed right there and wallowed in my apparent downfall. I could have seen it as something I couldn't recover from or fallen into a state of hopelessness, but my personal resolve and belief system would not allow it. I believed that I could indeed bounce back and so I again made up my mind that I would excel and do the work necessary to Make it Happen. For the next and last three semesters of my college career, my GPA started to rise significantly. The very next semester it climbed to 3.5, then to 3.75 and finally to 4.0 by the last semester. By the time I graduated, I had attained a more reputable cumulative GPA. It happened because of my faith & mindset.

Some people view faith strictly as a religious phenomenon, but I see it as being much more than that. Faith is the confidence that you can accomplish what you desire even when you can't see how, when the odds are against you. It's a mindset, like I've been saying throughout this chapter. It's knowing without a doubt that you will accomplish your established goals. It's an inner knowing, a belief. My faith is very strong. When I believe that something will happen as in the examples I've shared, I believe it wholeheartedly and it becomes a part of how I operate. For example, I could have believed my administrative colleague and waited to pursue my dream of becoming a principal, but that would go against my wiring. I could have chosen to believe that I would get lost in the system at a larger university, but I chose not to believe that way and in turn reaped the benefits of holding fast to my beliefs.

At some point in my life, I made up my mind that I was going to achieve certain goals and nothing stood in the way of making them happen. But let me warn you: Your dreams alone cannot get you anywhere in life. Your dreams must be accompanied with a strong belief system. You must believe that your dreams can become a reality. Anything I've ever desired in life started with a dream and a belief. But I couldn't stop at just believing. Your faith and beliefs are not fully operational without action accompanying them. For Christians, this may sound familiar, while for others this may be a new concept. Faith is nonexistent if you do not walk in it. What I mean by that is if we believe something, we must take steps towards making that something come true. If I had not started applying for principal jobs, one would likely not just fall into my lap. If I never entered the pageant, there's no way I would have received that crown. Belief requires action. You have to live out your beliefs in your actions.

St. Augustine said, "*Pray as though everything depended on God. Work as though everything depended on you.*" This is exactly what I'm saying. We need our works to spell out our faith. In order for us to move from belief to reality, there are some steps that must be taken. Faith is about believing what is not yet in existence. And like St. Augustine said, we might pray to God to make it a reality, but the work is our responsibility. It's like saying, "I believe I'm going to land my dream job with a lucrative salary and enviable benefits and perks," but you sit at home watching videos on your computer. How will any employer even know that you exist? You have to take action. You have to take the time away from your videos and draft a powerhouse resume or Curriculum Vitae and then find recruiters, headhunters, or direct individuals to send them out to help you land that coveted position. The job will never find you without your efforts to be found.

When I left my principal position to start my current company, Teach Educators & Scholars Organization, LLC, I had to have a lot of faith and I had to let my faith be larger than my fears. And trust me, there was plenty of reason to fear. The reality was stark. I was doing something I had never done before and it was a critical time in my life. For more than a year, I had been talking to my husband about leaving my post as principal. In my professional opinion, the timing was right. I had just removed the school from the state's lists of schools in need of improvement. I had accomplished what I set out to do. But leaving was risky, very risky. I earned half of the household income and we lived up to the limit. Our daughter was already in college and our son was in a private high school. The odds were stacked against me. As an entrepreneur I would no longer get a stable paycheck on the 15th and 30th of each month. The days ahead promised to be very tough and unpredictable. This is precisely why I didn't make a move right then.

Then one day, my superintendent grossly expanded my responsibilities and gave me an additional assignment to take on the role of Curriculum Supervisor in addition to being a school principal. That was a life changing day for me. I nearly cried as he added this additional responsibility onto my plate. I was appalled at first, but eventually I felt like this was an opportunity for me to prove myself again. Note the mindset shift. First I cried, feeling very overwhelmed by the assignment. It meant I had two full time jobs to fulfill. I initially thought that there was no way I could do both jobs and I wanted to run. However, seeing myself as overwhelmed didn't look good on me. I couldn't let the ship go down and I certainly couldn't allow myself to give into fear of failure.

I begrudgingly took the assignment, but I quickly had to change my mindset about how I would approach this new assignment. Obviously, the superintendent saw something in me that made him feel confident asking me to take on the assignment. I had to see the value in what I had to offer and how I could help move the district to a better place from a curriculum standpoint. I could continue to make a difference on an even broader level. And so I set out to do just that and spent my last year as principal working diligently to fulfill both roles to the best of my ability. I plugged away day in and day out. However, I didn't really enjoy doing both jobs at the same time. I could enjoy both separately, but together was not so enjoyable. There was a lot on my plate and I often left without finishing all that I set out to do. Unfortunately because of the nature of both positions, it became impossible for the work to ever be done exceptionally well. That type of work environment was not ideal for me and I found myself being overly tired, sleep deprived, stressed and ultimately dissatisfied. Here is when I began to dream again of more for myself and my professional future. I felt my call to step out on faith pulling me even harder than before accepting the dual positions.

The two positions were taking their toll on my physical health too, though I tried to hide it, but I was catching respiratory infections every other month, my neck and back injuries from 2002 were flaring up every chance they got and I soon realized I needed a change. I always thought that I would never retire from the school system, because I always had dreams beyond this. After taking on the new responsibilities, my days were spent in meeting after meeting. I had never attended so many meetings in my life. And this was to become my foreseeable future. This was never what I envisioned for my career. I enjoyed the interaction with staff and students and I loved when we were creating opportunities for students to succeed. I signed up to make a difference, which I had done by leading the school out of being in need of improvement status. But at this point in my career, a stark reality was being revealed. While I had previously been able to tap into my creative and innovative side to find the best approach to move the needle of school growth, those opportunities became fewer and fewer. The additional position shifted my focus and priorities greatly and I no longer felt that I was able to do that effectively. My time and attention were much more administrative and managerial at this point and I did not feel as productive nor energized. The biggest sign was the decline in my health.

Sometimes we ignore the physical or emotional clues that signal to us that our lives need something different. Sometimes we need to shift our focus and redirect our beliefs to the next stop on our journey. I tried not to notice what was happening physically and I tried to come up with excuses for why things were out of whack, so to speak, but deep down inside, I knew. Even my blood pressure was elevated. I typically have a blood pressure that is relatively low. At this point in my career, I was around 130 over 80. For me that was too high. Pay attention to your body. Your body doesn't lie and it will get your attention. Sometimes your body just tells you to rest, other times it may be screaming at you to make a life change. This was one such time for me. Luckily for me, I had been dreaming of my next step for well over a year. And I believed that I could make the dream a reality. I just needed to be in agreement with my husband, because I valued his opinion and support. Besides, this decision to leave my job would absolutely affect my household. Remember I was an equal breadwinner, so I needed to be able to prove to him and myself that I could do it. I really believed that I could do it.

Faith needs to override all other beliefs. It's especially helpful whenever you make major changes in your life, whenever you step outside of your comfort zone or whenever you do something you've never done before. Without strong faith, you may be faced with fears and doubts that keep you from moving forward. Even when you have a plan, fear can cloud your belief that you will succeed. Fear is the enemy! Combat fear with your faith and belief.

Fear is crippling and can keep you second guessing yourself and even cause you to believe something contrary to what you want to believe as in the time my faith was really tested. I was less than one year into running and operating my own business and I was not succeeding. I was hardly earning any money and I was...no my household was in trouble. My mortgage was late and I had NEVER been late paying my mortgage and unfortunately, I couldn't even sell my house to fix the situation. My house was under water. The housing market in NJ plummeted like in most states and I was stuck. I tried to talk to my mortgage company about alternative arrangements, but none were panning out for me and I was digging a wider and deeper hole. My worse fears were coming true and I didn't know what to do. My thoughts and beliefs were getting clouded by my circumstances and I was not demonstrating faith.

I sat kneeling on the side of my bed, letting the reality sink in that I was officially in foreclosure and was suddenly overwhelmed with grief. I let out a wail that expressed my overpowering sense of failure, stress and helplessness. I did not know what I was going to do. Thoughts of guilt flooded my mind as I replayed every negative word ever spoken about leaving the security of my job. I was now to blame for my family's demise and I didn't have a clue as to how to bounce back. The denial letter was resting on the bed and my husband sat beside me rubbing my back whispering something that was supposed to be consoling, but all I felt was despair. My faith had been rocked and I didn't have an answer for how to turn the situation around. I wept uncontrollably for what seemed liked hours, giving in to all of my suppressed fears, but then my husband reminded me of words I had spoken months before. He said, "You have to look at what's in your **faith**, not what's in your **face**!" And just like that, I had to stop and look at him...questions in my eyes, yet an inner knowing that he was right. It was as though those words were magic. I made a decision. I immediately dried my tears and leaned in to what I knew was true. My faith was way stronger than my fears and my present circumstances. I was going to come out of this situation and I was going to be able to tell others about it.

That evening was a turning point for me. Those reassuring, yet poignant words were exactly what I needed to hear and the timing could not have been better. I had just won a major battle against fear and it was with my best weapon, faith. Faith caused me to begin to see my way clear out of this momentary downfall. I would not allow a denial letter to defeat me and I decided my faith and beliefs would be the impetus for change. As time would have it, we were able to get a modification on our loan and I learned new lessons on how to run and operate a small business.

My belief system has to be powerful in order for me to overcome the biggest obstacle of fear. Holding onto your beliefs and faith do not mean that things won't go wrong. Anything can happen. That's life. Faith becomes the lens through which you have to judge your situations and circumstances. What's in your face can discourage you and even distract you from the mission of fulfilling your dreams. There are enough distractions without having to deal with fear. And what exactly are you fearful of? Are you afraid of failure or are you afraid of success? Are you afraid of rejection or ridicule?

Fear is a defeatist mindset. It reveals what you really believe. When I had my meltdown that fateful night, I was most afraid of failure. I was afraid that if I failed at business, my family would suffer, my kids wouldn't be able to go to school, my business would have to close and people would look at me differently, especially that I've always been known to be successful. This episode made me come face to face with my greatest fears. Thankfully, I didn't stay there. I had to change my self-talk and calm the voices in my head that tried to compel me to give in to fear. Sure, I wallowed for a few minutes, but ultimately, my faith was stronger. I knew deep down inside that I was not a failure, I just had not reached success yet. I had to change my narrative to one of courage.

Courage is when you do something in spite of how you might feel and in spite of your fears. I had to pick myself up with a renewed mindset and get back to work. I began to work as though everything depended on me all the while I was praying to God for help. I sat down and looked at what I was doing and what I could be doing. I started tapping into my creativity and innovation and took another step of faith, which led to the birth of my tutoring program. At the time, I was tutoring five students, though it was never what I intended when I started my business. My goal was to create an educational consulting firm where I provided professional development training and consulting services to schools and educational organizations. But, there was a need for quality tutoring services too.

I looked into starting a franchise tutoring business but I really could not afford it, so I studied different tutoring business models and set out to create my own. This opened up another stream of income that I never dreamed nor imagined until the situation presented itself to me. I was on to something. One thing I've noticed over the years is that if I put action with my faith/belief and start operating as though I want something new to happen, eventually something starts to happen.

It's really amazing to me how faith and belief combined with action have changed my life and my business. The action steps that follow belief are equivalent to a farmer planting seeds in one season and reaping the harvest in another season. That's always what happens to me. I plant seeds of belief by actively working to make my dreams a reality and then in the due season, I am able to reap in the form of new business. It's really quite amazing.

When you finally begin to take those faith steps and start working towards your dream (even in the face of seeing nothing happening), you have to make a decision. Decisions are necessary to keep you moving in the right direction. You have to decide to work. When you don't make decisions, you are in the place of indecision and I can tell you from experience that being in the place of indecision is very stressful and well...indecisive. It leaves you feeling unsettled and uncertain which paralyzes you from moving forward towards fulfilling your destiny. Making a decision to move forward with a laser like focus is important to feeding your belief that you can accomplish your set goals.

## Tonya's Take Aways

**There is power in positive thinking. There is power in your belief system. There is power in your mindset. There is power in your faith. As you are pursuing living your dreams, you need to be in touch with your faith and beliefs. If they are not right, replace them. Your faith is what can catapult your life, career or business to a new level. Without faith and a positive mindset, you hinder your progress. But your dreams and faith alone will not get you to success, you have to take steps, make moves, do something tangible to support your belief system. Your actions demonstrate what you actually believe. You can do great things with powerful beliefs and actions.**

# 5 BUILD STRONG RELATIONSHIPS

"Remember, the first year is the year you don't make any changes. Just focus on getting to know your people." This was advice given to me when I became a principal. That first year was a whirlwind, so much to learn, so much to do. When I was training in graduate school, we were told one of the first things we do as administrators is to develop a vision, but helpful advisors had another idea. I had to reconcile the two ideas to find what made the most sense for me. I chose developing relationships. This proved to be easier said than done.

When I inherited the mostly veteran team of teachers, I learned that they were not loyal to me just because I was their new administrator. In fact, the only ones who were loyal to me were the ones who I hired when I started. The others were either loyal to their former leader or each other. I had a lot of work to do and it didn't stop with the teachers. I had to connect with the parents in the school community, many of whom may not have always felt welcomed and I had to develop relationships with the students who had no idea what to think of me. My position alone, would not help me become a successful principal. I needed everybody to help me attain this.

You might remember that I was hired to lead a school in need of improvement. That meant they were essentially a failing school. The morale was low and though they were very dedicated and committed, the teachers were overwhelmed. I was very different from my predecessor and I had my work cut out for me. Luckily for me because they were so dedicated, many of them showed up in the summer at the first sight of an open and ready building to begin the process of decorating their classrooms for the new school year. This was my opportunity to initiate establishing a rapport. I made it a priority to sit down with as many of them as possible to start the relationship-building process. I realized there was no way I was going to have any success without them being on board, buying into my vision and essentially doing the work to change our circumstances.

Those initial conversations were very interesting. Many of them had been there for years and had strong opinions about the school and its community. It became clear how much of an outsider I was with my different views and approaches to leadership. They were not accustomed to my style. The staff had their own preconceived notions of how things should be done relying on tradition and previous experiences. Some showed resistance to me initially, while others sat back and simply watched my every move, sometimes with a critical eye. In the beginning, there seemed to be an "us vs. them" mentality that seemed to infiltrate the place and the only thing that was going to change this was developing a trusting relationship with them.

WIFM? Do these letters look familiar to you? They stand for "What's in it for me?" People want to know what they stand to gain from connecting with you. It doesn't matter whether you are in a personal dating relationship, a friendship, a working relationship, a partnering business relationship, networking or leading others as in my example. People do not want to waste their time or effort on somebody they do not know who may not have their best interests at heart. They want to be aligned to people who are going to help them succeed and not hinder them.

Unfortunately, I have experience with misalignment. When I became a principal, there was one thing I was certain of and that was I didn't want to be anything like my first administrator. She was a bully, not at all somebody I wanted to be aligned to, but I couldn't choose my supervisor. I met her during my first year as a new teacher. From all accounts, she didn't enjoy a great reputation among staff nor students and it wasn't long before I joined in their assessment of her. She never really tried to get to know me and it seemed that whenever she did have something to say to me it was negative. She once yelled at me for teaching grammar in isolation. As a new teacher who was still enrolled in my education coursework, I didn't yet have a full grasp of what she was telling me not to do, nor did I know the rationale for it. I had a lot to learn about best practices. The last thing I needed as a new teacher was for my supervisor, who could have shown support and mentoring, to attack me verbally, but she did.

Her antics didn't stop with just yelling at me. She actually put her hands on me one day when she walked down the hall overhearing part of a conversation I was having with a colleague. She decided she didn't like what she thought she heard me saying about my teaching and approached me, took her index and middle fingers and thumped them on the side of my head saying something to the effect, "...when are you going to get it through your thick skull, blah, blah, blah..." I never heard her fully complete her rant because I was fuming! It was all I could do to keep from knocking her out right then and there in the center of the school hallway in the middle of the school day. I seethed, speechless, fists tightly clutched, as I tried to remain calm. *Who does that? Who gets physical with their staff?* I'd never seen anything like it and although I wanted to, I didn't retaliate. I managed to disappear down the hall without incident, but I had no respect for her after that.

This wasn't the last of her shenanigans. She seemed to have it out for me. I remember submitting my hand written lesson plans to her (It was the late 90's) and she verbally ripped me to pieces. The apparent problem was not that I had written the plans by hand, but rather she just decided I was the one to pick on that day, or at least that was my take on it. I left her office annoyed and decided to put her to the test. She wanted me to change the plans, which I knew were absolutely fine, and so I redid the lesson plans, except I only typed them up very neatly, but I refused to change the content one bit. I knew there was no problem with what I had planned. They were very thoughtful and appropriate for my students. I also knew that she would scrutinize them so I took great care to plan activities that were appropriate. She had no idea that I was testing her. She saw the new presentation of the lesson plans and praised me for the content and tried to make a big deal about what I had prepared for my students. It was unbelievable! She just proved what I already knew was the issue. As you might imagine, I limited the amount of time I spent in her presence. She had a toxic personality. By this point, it was apparent that she was not there to help me succeed. After the completion of that school year, I requested a transfer. If she had taken the time to cultivate a relationship with me, I would have probably had a more successful school year. She created unnecessary tension.

**The 3rd Principle is to Build Strong Relationships.** The strength of relationships can affect the success of organizations and individuals. It's to everyone's benefit to develop strong, healthy relationships. Developing healthy relationships may not always be easy because relationships are comprised of people and people are complex, even more so when they are in relationships. However, when they exist, it makes a difference. Like most people, I highly value positive relationships with others.

Relationships serve different purposes depending on the circumstances. They are important for both personal and professional reasons because they offer the following:

- ☐ Support
- ☐ Partnership
- ☐ Accountability
- ☐ Mentorship
- ☐ Companionship
- ☐ Opportunity to help others

So let's explore these a little further.

This year my husband and I celebrated 25 years of marriage. We went all out too, we had a vow renewal at a beautiful country club with the golf course as the backdrop to our wedding gazebo. A reception followed and later we went on a second Honeymoon. It was literally a dream come true for me. It was everything I hoped for and then some. We had an intimate gathering of family and friends – no more than 75 people. Our children stood up for us, our pastors (husband/wife team) performed the ceremony and we basked in the love that filled the atmosphere.

It might as well have been a wedding ceremony as we had a coordinator, wrote and exchanged heartfelt vows declaring our love and recommitting ourselves to one another for the remainder of our lives. Our reception included a DJ, live performances from both of our young adult children, toasts from loved ones, food and dancing. The colors were silver (for the 25 years) and raspberry. My silver, jewel-studded dress had all of the elegance of a new bride and my husband's silver tuxedo accentuated the elegance and merriment of the day.

But the celebration was about the 25 year marital relationship we've had with one another. If you know anybody who has been married for 25 years or even if you've been married that long, you know that to be able to spend that kind of time with somebody takes work. In a marriage, most of the aforementioned relationship purposes listed, come into play. Marriages should start out as a friendship either prior to or during the dating phase of the relationship. Here, you get to know one another and develop an attachment, regard and care for each other. The bond becomes noticeably special and has the potential to grow. When it does grow into a dating relationship, you become companions and you enjoy a certain level of togetherness and closeness. You are likely found spending increasingly more time in each other's presence, talking frequently and thinking about one another. The nature of the relationship involves a developing partnership of sorts where you have each other's interests at heart and you are willing to do anything for one another and make decisions that benefit one another.

As the relationship grows, marriage can likely become the next phase of the relationship which brings with it a new level of involvement and commitment. At this point in the relationship, you have love for one another and you are often willing to die for the other. The stakes are much higher now and this partnership means more than it did previously. Now you are accountable to one another for your whereabouts, spending, thought process and other areas. It is generally natural and easy to support one another and wish the best for each other in whatever you endeavor to do. You have daily opportunities to demonstrate love and care for one another and this relationship becomes your most important relationship, even surpassing the one you may have had with your parents.

You hold each other in high esteem and respect and will often push one another to become the best you can be. You're thoughtful towards one another and you share many memories, laughter, experiences, good and bad times. Yet through all of the experiences, you don't waiver in your love for one another.

This example of a healthy marital relationships could serve as a model for other types of relationships as it has so many similar descriptive components. For example, in business relationships, you need to establish a rapport that is mutually beneficial for both, a partnership. You also need to demonstrate a measure of accountability and support, depending on the nature and depth of the business relationship. Trust must also be present if you are to help one another grow your businesses. It can be like a marriage of sorts.

Having been married for over 25 years, I've learned a lot about myself in relation to others. I've grown in character, confidence, maturity, spirituality, faith, commitment, dependability, accountability, persuasiveness, patience, faithfulness, loyalty, self-control, appreciation, service and I'm sure there are many more qualities that I cannot think of at the moment. These same character traits have been significant in developing relationships outside of marriage. They've helped me transfer these characteristics into developing friendships, business relationships, in teams that

I've led and with acquaintances I've met. I'm fortunate to have been able to see growth and use it in other situations.

When I served as a new principal, the relationships I built had certain parameters that I had to be mindful of at all times. These relationships would not mirror a marital relationship in terms of intimacy and commitment, but I did have the option to either make the relationships personal, and still be professional or I could have kept them strictly professional. I chose the former. Navigating how to relate to the people I supervised had to be somewhat strategic. I knew that as a leader, I would not have as much success with moving my vision forward without getting my staff to buy into my vision and join me in fulfilling it. The type of relationships I needed with my staff had to be authentic, genuine and safe. I needed them and they needed me.

I had to have a real connection with each of them. This connection had to be developed over a period of months and years as I spent time with them, got to know them, and showed appreciation to them for their talents and contributions to the success of students. I had to learn about what they valued and take care of their needs by providing support and necessary resources to help make their jobs easier. I had to be a good listener and I had to value them as professionals. Of course, I had my favorites, but all of them were essential to moving the needle of student achievement.

Allow me to paint a picture of how I nurtured and cultivated these personal, yet professional relationships in my role as a school leader. When my staff came to work each day, I made it a point to greet them as they entered the main office. I would chat with them about their students or their parents, special programming we had going on during the day or about their personal families. I was consistently congenial and light hearted in my approach. I made sure I was visible during the day and responsive to them if they called on me for help with students. I kept lines of communication open and made sure they were kept apprised of any news or information that was relevant.

I tried to create a fun, engaging environment, with a culture of support. I can recall one fall morning when the students were not coming in because of parent/teacher conferences; I cooked breakfast for my staff and gave away door prizes. This later became an annual event. I would bring in a lady who gave them shoulder rubs and light massages in the staff lounge to show my appreciation. We developed a closer bond as time passed. I also supported fun activities that they wanted to plan for students on special occasions and I made myself available to participate. We developed a warm, collegial atmosphere and it was a nice place to go to every morning. I almost always accommodated their requests to leave early because of family circumstances and I never made a big deal about it. I had an open door policy so that staff always felt welcomed to stop in whenever they wanted to chat. I was very intentional about developing a culture/climate that was inviting and welcoming for staff, students and community members.

As a leader, I made myself available and I didn't ask them to do what I wasn't willing to do myself. If I needed them to be trained on a particular topic, I also engaged in the training. I would serve lunch to students if we were short of staff and I wasn't afraid to pick up trash, wash down tables and the like. If I asked them to help students get excited about reading and writing, I did the same. I used my personal time to run a before school reading club for students. My staff quickly saw that I was invested and genuine. They began to develop trust in me and felt safe with me. I made it a point for them to know that I had their best interests at heart and that I was not against them, but rather for them and their success.

I spent time getting to know about them personally as well. I wanted to show them that I cared about them as people and about what they cared about. It was not always about me, it had to be about them as well and they needed to know it. I took opportunities to show them that I appreciated them and I made sure they had a voice to express what they felt and thought. They mattered to the overall operation and success of the organization. I needed them to be effective and they needed me to support them in the process. My relationships grew stronger and more meaningful over time.

If you find that you are in a position of leadership over a group of people, it's important that you think about the kind of relationship you want to have with them. You can choose to keep it strictly professional, but that can make it more challenging to get their complete support when you need it. That type of relationship may be more about compliance, doing what you need them to do and little more. When you personalize the professional relationship, you show your human side and make it more welcoming and possible for people to want to connect with and work with you.

Have you ever had a boss who kept it strictly business? If so, you may not have enjoyed the best relationship. Sure you might have respected him/her and even admired them for their accomplishments or contributions to the organization, but you knew that you would only get but so close to him/her. They likely didn't show you the care and concern that could have been shown in a more personal relationship. And when you needed something, you may have been more hesitant to approach him/her.

Leaders who enjoy the greatest success fulfilling their goals and moving the organization forward to meet their mission and realize their vision need to be Level 4 or 5 leaders according the John Maxwell's, **5 Levels of Leadership.** Maxwell is a well-known leadership expert, author and speaker whose book talks about 5 different levels of leadership. The first level is people follow you simply because you hold the title. That's the Position level. No leader wants to remain at Level 1. By the time you reach Level 4, people follow you because of what you have done for them and at Level 5, people follow you because of who you are and what you represent. Levels 4 and 5 leaders develop more meaningful relationships with their people, that's the only way they can get to these levels. They understand the importance of strong relationships in fulfilling their organizational purpose. Our relationships as leaders can make or break the success of an organization.

But what if you are not a leader of an organization but you are someone with dreams to do something new and different in your life? How do relationships matter in your case? First of all, no man is an island. We need each other to live and succeed in all aspects of life. Anything I've ever done in life required people with different experiences to connect with me. You need people who are going to be in your corner providing you with the support that you need. You need people to give you life, not those who suck the life out of you. These are the people who help you on your journey towards fulfilling your dreams and God-given purpose.

When I became a new teacher in the late 90's, I was coming into the profession with a background in social services and a

Bachelor's Degree in Psychology. I earned my teacher's certificate through an alternate route path my state had for those who had degrees in fields other than education. Because I did not go through a formal teacher preparation program with student teaching, I was not as prepared as the classroom teacher who had gone through the training. I had a lot to learn! I was eager to learn and I was excited about the opportunity of working with students. I was required to take education coursework, provided by some of the local universities, which I did simultaneous to starting my teaching assignment. I was also assigned a mentor teacher, who made a huge difference for me. She gave me life because she believed in my success and demonstrated it in her support. She was the ideal mentor.

She was a retired teacher and she had worked with a demographic similar to the one that I was assigned. I'll never forget one of the most meaningful conversations I had with her after she observed my teaching. I was struggling and I couldn't really hide it. She reassured me that I was doing fine, but needed to put some strategies in practice to help me have a greater impact in the classroom. For example, I assumed that because my students were older (7th graders), they should know what was expected at their age and stage. My mentor told me that I needed to explicitly explain everything to my students, prepare them for everything that was coming next and offer visuals for those who needed the added support. She also told me to put predictable routines in place for them because it provided them with consistency. It was so simple, yet very effective. She made herself available to me whenever I had questions and needed support.

This mentoring relationship was different than other relationships because it was more professional, yet had elements of the personal. For one, she did not evaluate me so that made the relationship less stressful and offered safety for me to make and learn from my mistakes as a new teacher. It provided a cushion for me to fall on when I had concerns. Her experience alone was very valuable to me as a new teacher. She provided me with the support every new teacher needs when they are starting out their careers.

Years later, I was able to pay it forward when I agreed to be the collaborative teacher for a student teacher from the local college. She was actually older than me, but was entering the profession after having raised her children. She was a very kind lady, nurturing and warm. She was also very shy when she started. I'll never forget when she taught her first independent lesson. She was very nervous and scared. My role was to model good teaching, support and encourage her by giving her feedback. The principal decided that he was going to randomly stop by the classroom for an observation. He didn't know that she was going to be teaching the lesson. I immediately stepped to the door and asked him to please come back another day. She was doing her first lesson and his presence would be disastrous. He obliged and she was able to continue without the scrutiny. When I gave her feedback, it was invaluable to her and non-threatening. My role as a mentor was to support and give her feedback as she launched her new career. It made a difference. Having finished her coursework and 10 years of teaching, she is very good at what she does and enjoys a very positive reputation.

A mentoring relationship is not usually as personal as a good friendship, although it can be. The mentoring relationship is meaningful, and has the goal of helping another with personal or professional development. The mentor serves in the capacity of one with expertise and is a guide. Mentors do what they do out of the goodness of their hearts because they care about helping others.

I've been blessed to serve as a mentor for a number of people and I cannot stress how rewarding it is for me to give back to others in this capacity. I mentioned one of my mentees previously in this book. Even though it has been over 20 years since I first mentored this young woman, we are still very much involved in each other's lives. I love her like my own daughter or little sister. She is a remarkable woman whom I believe the world will one day be introduced to and fall in love with. She will make her mark on this earth and that will be life changing for others. Now our relationship is primarily personal and I seldom have to be the mentor to her. We have a mutual understanding to just be there for one another. Recently, I was able to reach out to her for support and advice on a matter and she was very accommodating and helpful. During that same conversation, she mentioned that had I not come into her life at the time I did, she would not be the woman she is today. Your relationship as a mentor is substantial to another's success in life, career or business.

As a business owner, I have had to learn how to leverage relationships with those I do not know very well. Oftentimes I find myself in environments with other entrepreneurs or business owners. At first it was like being dropped in the middle of the deep end of the pool without a life jacket and being told to sink or swim. It was overwhelming for me, scary even. I didn't really know how to work a room and would find myself looking for the one and only familiar face and monopolizing his or her time. I seldom ventured out into the room to see if I could make the acquaintance of others. I would find reasons to go to the lady's room or look for the service staff for another hors d'oeuvre or act like I needed to take an important phone call.

Eventually, these events became slightly more comfortable, but my ease with introducing myself and making small talk was limiting. It was not uncommon for you to see me with a pocket full of business cards, passing them out like candy on

Halloween and collecting as many as I could and then leaving satisfied that I "networked", only to never see nor hear from the card holder ever again.

I had a lot to learn about networking and leveraging relationships with those I met for the first time at similar events. I didn't know that my interaction needed to be about what I could do for them, not what they could do for me. After meeting someone new, I needed to learn how to find out enough information about what they did and who they were, as time allowed, so that I could either find an opportunity to connect them with others who could benefit from what they had to offer, give them my business, or propose an idea for partnership and/or collaboration. It took me a couple of years to figure out the benefits of networking and developing new relationships.

Typically, there is seldom enough time to cultivate meaningful relationships in the initial meeting, but there is always an opportunity to set aside additional time to meet at a later date. Soon I realized the value of following up with those that I'd meet at a conference or similar event. I've become a pro now...I'm very comfortable in any environment, even if I know no one. I have developed the savvy needed to talk to people, establish a rapport and almost always walk away feeling richer from the experience. I now welcome networking opportunities because I know that I have a chance to associate with someone new and perhaps build my and their business as a result of our meeting.

Earlier this year, I was interested in meeting people who have successful speaking businesses as I was preparing to officially launch the speaking side to my business. So I decided to reach out to a well-known international speaker via his website and he was gracious enough to set aside time to talk to me for over one full hour. In fact, we talked twice for over an hour. It was absolutely eye opening for me and he connected me to another gentleman who walked me through a technique they both used to make new connections through online networking. The second gentleman actually walked me through using a very popular professional online social media platform to link up with new people in the industries that were of interest to me. I sent them all similar messages where I highlighted something from their online profiles that spoke to me and then I told them that I'd like to hear about their journeys to becoming professional speakers and asked them if they were amenable to talking with me.

To my pleasant surprise, the majority of those I reached out to said yes! I had some rich conversations with some very generous public speakers. While talking to them, they were honored to be approached by me and reveled in being able to share their stories. It was enlightening for me and helped me in my planning process. It was through these conversations that I solidified my need to finally sit down and write this book. They offered great advice and insight into the speaking industry. This online networking turned out to be far better than I could have ever imagined. It also opened up an opportunity for collaboration and new relationships with some. Networking either in person or online can open doors for meaningful relationships. Network with a purpose and with a goal to help someone else.

When you are looking to "Make it Happen" in your life, career or business, it's important that you have a relationship with someone who can hold you accountable for setting and reaching your goals and objectives. Accountability partners can either be someone you know very well or someone you may not know well, but hold in high esteem. Your accountability partner needs to be someone who you give permission to push you and question you about what you are doing as it relates to your goals. This person will be holding you accountable for your actions and motives as it relates to what you've committed to accomplishing.

Depending on what you are trying to accomplish, your accountability partner may coach you, give you assignments to complete, challenge you and help you reach your goals. When I started my business in 2011, I had an accountability partner. She is a very good friend of mine who is also an entrepreneur with a M.B.A. She is a wealth of knowledge who loves and cares about me, which makes her a champion for my success and someone who is always in my corner. We probably talked 5 out of 7 days per week and she challenged me, pushed me, critiqued me, praised me and supported me through the start-up phase and she was essentially a blessing to me. I don't know how I would have gotten through that phase without her. She held me to my goals and expectations without giving in to the fact that we were friends. She was a God-send and I cannot imagine having started my business without her.

As you can see, there are a number of reasons behind why you need strong relationships. Relationships can either be life-giving or stressful depending on the dynamics. So it's very important that we cultivate and build positive, healthy relationships that can be mutually beneficial to all. Studies have shown that people who build strong social relationships live on average significantly longer than those who do not.

**Tonya's Takeaways:**

**Be circumspect in the people you align yourself to as you want people who are going to help you rather than hinder you. Relationship building, both personal and professional, is critical to your success as you venture to do something new and different in your life, career or business.**

# 6 BE DRIVEN & DETERMINED

"I did it! I did it!" I couldn't believe it! I had run the whole 3.2 miles without walking and I couldn't wait to share the big news with my biggest supporter and champion. Tears streamed down my cheeks as I pushed the numbers on my cell phone to call my husband. I love sharing news with him. I'd been running all summer, working ambitiously through my couch to 5k app and for the first time ever, I had finally reached my goal. I had accomplished what seemed like a huge feat to me. I could barely catch my breath as I shouted through the receiver that I had done it! "I ran all the way!" I could barely contain my enthusiasm. You would have thought that I had won a race or I placed in the top ten in my age category, but none of these were the case. I won my own race against myself, against my mindset, against my apprehension and against my own inner voice that kept wanting me to give up. I had reached my first goal!

When I was 15 & 16 years old, I ran high school track. I wasn't very fast, but I wasn't slow either. I was fast enough to be on the varsity track team and that was satisfying to me. My race at the time was the half mile. I had also run the quarter mile and the 2 mile (which I hated). I did moderately well, enough to earn a Letter in track & field. After my junior year in high school, my running days ceased. I became pre-occupied with life and never really gave it much thought or time. Let's fast forward to nearly a few decades later when I started contemplating healthy alternatives. Others around me were picking up running and trying to reverse the hands of time on health and fitness. I figured, why not?

I reminisced about my glory days on the cinder track and wondered whether I could go back when a close friend, who was fighting a major disease, shared how she turned to running to boost her health and fitness and combat some of the effects of the disease. She encouraged me to do the same and painted a picture that made me believe that running was a real possibility for me too. She recommended I download an app on my phone that would take me from sitting on the couch to running a solid 5k. I decided it wouldn't hurt to find and download the app. I had nothing to lose.

I went out for the first "run". It was embarrassing to say the least. I was winded a moment after the app told me to start running. I was only able to run approximately the length of one house on my street before I was out of breath and my legs were burning with pain. It was ridiculous! Can you imagine the thoughts that crossed my mind? *What do you think you're doing? You're too old for this! You can't do this, it's way too hard! How do you expect to run 5k if you can't even make it a few yards?* I really wanted to turn around and go back home, but something inside would not let me. If my friend could do it, why couldn't I? Although I wasn't fighting for my health like she was, I still had to push through the pain, the negative self-defeating thoughts and keep moving. And that's exactly what I did, I pushed every day for weeks until it became easier to run the length of a house, then two houses, a block and eventually the entirety of the 3.2 miles.

This became an internal fight for me and it paralleled life in so many ways. It took me a few months before I could run the entire 5k without walking. And the journey was tough. Every single day I ran required an internal pep talk to get me out there so I can work towards reaching my goals. There were times that the app would direct me to conquer more distance and I didn't feel I was ready, so I had to repeat some days so that I could build up my endurance and strength. I didn't have any running partners, which for me worked well. This was something I had to do myself. I had to combat my negative thoughts and prove something to myself. I needed to show myself that I could set out to do something that was going to be very challenging and actually accomplish what I set out to do. This would prove to have an impact on my business.

I was implementing the **4<sup>th</sup> Power Principle – Be Determined and Driven.** This personal lesson in drive and determination proved very beneficial as I was also in the process of building my small business. I was still in the early stages of the business and I needed to defeat the odds that most small businesses don't make it to 5 years before needing to close their doors. Each day I got out there to run was a victory for me. It showed me the value of fighting to make it happen. And believe me it was a fight! There were days that I struggled to get my breathing pattern working for me. *Breathe in through the nose and out the mouth or is it breath through the mouth and out the nose?* And then there were the leg pains. The legs would burn, sometime the shins would feel like they were splitting into two and other days it felt like my feet were going to give out on me. I still battled lower back problems and many days I would be reminded of my injury. Between the breathing, pain and thoughts, I had a reason every single day to give up and never go back to running outside again.

It would have been easy to quit because nobody was really watching me. But I had integrity and that outweighed the desire to give up and put away my sneakers for good. I had to have a certain commitment and drive to do something so challenging. I believe that anything in life worth having is worth fighting for. That statement can apply to many circumstances, including relationships, jobs, school, business, personal accomplishments like running a 5k and any other goal you might set out to do. For me, it also applied to my small business.

Drive and determination are synonymous with words like persistence, ambitious, conquer, eagerness, striving, passionate, thirst, desire and yearning. These words carry a punch, they are strong. They make me want to move, to push and not stop until I reach my goals or my dreams. To achieve anything worth achieving takes commitment. Mario Andretti, a famous, multi-award winning retired race car driver said this, *"Desire is the key to motivation, but it's determination and commitment to an unrelenting pursuit of your goal – a commitment to excellence – that will enable you to attain the success you seek."*

Andretti's words could not be truer. How else do you think successful people make things happen? They need to first have a yearning desire to do something new and different. They have to want it badly enough to make the next move. The same is true for you. We spent the previous chapters talking about your purpose and the dreams you have to fulfill your purpose. We talked about the mindset you need to believe that you can indeed realize your dreams and we talked about the importance of being strategically aligned to the right people to help you make it happen. Now I want to ask you? How badly do you want it? How badly do you want to see your dreams come true? Can you see it? Can you feel it? Can you almost touch it? What are you willing to do for it? Are you willing to do what it takes? Are you willing to be unstoppable? Because that's what it may take for you to change the status quo and realize your dreams.

Drive and determination come easy for some people, but not for all. Many people need to be motivated or need to combat the enemies to drive and determination. You may need to combat these enemies. Some of the enemies include procrastination, excuses, fear of stepping out of comfort zones, fear of taking risks or failure. I'm sure you can name more excuses and enemies, but these are plenty. Which enemy is keeping you from moving forward with pursuing your dreams?

Let's address procrastination because it is very common. It is the opposite of discipline. We procrastinate when we give attention to something else that seems better in the moment than the task that is being avoided. Your reason for procrastinating may have something to do with the other enemies listed above or you may have other reasons for why you procrastinate. No matter the reason, the effect is the same...things are not getting done. Can you think of a time that you wish you had not procrastinated on a task because you could have been further along, had you started sooner? What if your goal is to build up your investment portfolio yet you let months or years go by before you open up your account? You are losing money! The longer you wait to start something, the longer it takes for you to be on your journey. If I waited until I was ready to start my business, I would never have started. I would still be trying to get things off the ground four years later and I'd be no place at all.

For some reason you think that there's always tomorrow or the next day to start working towards your goal, but you are delaying starting your new life, business or career and you may also be losing out on potential opportunities. Most people need time to start something new in their lives. If you are trying to start a new career, you need a killer resume and job leads to pursue. Waiting could cause you to miss out on current opportunities. With the competitive nature of the job market, I would recommend you not procrastinate. Waiting could be the difference between your getting the position you want or someone else beating you to it.

Procrastination is also a mindset issue, much like everything else. What lies are you telling yourself about working towards fulfilling your dreams? What beliefs do you have about your reality? Do you believe strongly that you can do what it is you dream of doing? What's stopping you? Where is your drive?

Where is your hunger for something new? Where is your passion? It's time to stop hiding behind the excuse of procrastination. Either you want a change or you do not! You decide. As long as you continue to put off what you can do today tomorrow, you lose, and so do those who stand to benefit from what you have to offer.

You've got to be persistent and unstoppable when it comes to pursuing your destiny! No one can make you move, but you have to have the desire and faith to take the necessary steps towards living it. How will you discipline yourself? Perhaps you need to take small steps towards your dream, but discipline yourself to make consistent steps daily or weekly towards making moves. Schedule your actions and don't waiver from following through. Push yourself, motivate yourself, surround yourself with people who will join you in your quest. Make a commitment to yourself and those around you to never give up. Even though taking small steps may take longer than big steps, at least you are moving in the right direction. It's certainly easier to get to California (from New Jersey) by plane, but if I choose to drive from the east coast to the west coast, I'm still going to get to my destination, it's just going to take me longer. The same is true for you. If you decide to drive to your destiny, that's okay, just get in the car!

Just as procrastination is an excuse, there are other excuses that you allow yourself to make that keep you from being driven towards your goals. Those excuses are often rehearsed in your head or they are spoken out loud. Either way, they are the lies you tell yourself to keep you stagnant. Lies like, *"I'm not good enough, I don't have enough education, I don't have the money, I don't have time, My kids keep me too busy, People might reject me, I don't know where to begin, It's too hard, I might not succeed or People might laugh at me,"* are usually steeped in the insecurities you hold about yourself. You may even be able to rationalize each of them and put up a great argument as to why they are legitimate, but recognize them for what they are. They are also the enemies to drive and determination. If you want to make a change or transformation in your life, you've got to examine your thinking and evaluate your drive.

Drive and determination suggest that you are willing to do what it takes to make your dreams a reality. And why wouldn't you want to do that with your dreams? Why would you continue to let days, weeks, months or even years go by without you going after what you want? You've got to combat your excuses by making a decision to take action. Replace each negative, self-defeating, sabotaging thought with thoughts of action, positivity and movement. You need to take captive every thought that is keeping you from your destiny. That means recognize and acknowledge when they creep into your mind and give them a different assignment and replace them with better thoughts. When you give in to the excuses or the fears, you are giving up a life of satisfaction and fulfillment! Fear has a way of keeping you bound, paralyzing you and holding you back from moving forward. You need to see fear as the enemy to your purpose. This enemy wants you to stay away from the life God has created for you! Once you recognize the enemy, you can defeat it! Defeat comes with a DECISION! You have to decide that you will no longer listen to the lies in your head and you have to decide that you are going to take the steps that are needed to walk into your destiny.

While you are on your journey, you may find there is a lot for you to learn about yourself or about your drive and determination. Sometimes it's helpful to have people in your life who can point out lessons for you as well. When I was training for the 5K, I often had conversations with my accountability partner. During one of those conversations where I was bragging about my 5K accomplishments, she pointed out to me the parallel between my running and my building my business. There were several factors that contributed to my drive and determination to succeed at both. For one, when I started running, I had to have a clear vision to see the end goal, which was to run the entire 3.2 miles without walking. Similarly, in business, I had to have a clear vision to see an end goal...which at the time was to build a strong consulting, training and tutoring business.

Once I started running, I had to have knowledge of the direction I would need to take to make progress. I mapped out that path in my neighborhood and also a nearby park where I could get in the required distance throughout the program. Similarly, in business I had to have direction as to how I was going to get to my end goal of having a successful consulting and training business. I also realized that sometimes my vision was not clear in my business, which made my journey more challenging. These are the times that I had to pause and make changes. I was careful though not to allow it to distract me. I continued to act with drive.

To get out there most days and start running required another factor that paralleled nicely to my business and that was the need to be fearless. I admit, it was quite scary going out there, especially in the beginning, and running, knowing that it had been nearly three decades, knowing that I was out of shape, knowing that I might not have been fully prepared for what was ahead, but I stepped out there and did it! I started in spite of potential excuses I could have made and I kept going. That same fearlessness is needed when you start a new business. It's scary not being an experienced business owner with limited resources and limited knowledge of running and operating a business. But I was baptized by fire by jumping in with both feet and taking a major faith walk to do something different and new. I had to have a willingness to take risks and step outside of my comfort zone. You must be willing to do the same.

Running was risky for me...I had previous injuries, I didn't know if I could actually handle the stress on my body. And getting out there at my age and stage in life was also very uncomfortable for me. But, I did it. I didn't know if I would succeed, but I was determined and committed to the task of getting out there each week to run the designated distance for the day, even when I was unsure of each incremental increase in distance. The same existed in operating a small business, I took a major risk walking into the uncertainty of financial stability. I was way outside my comfort zone because everything had to be created from its inception, nothing already existed that was to be. I didn't necessarily have a blueprint for success, I was making it up as I went along and that was very risky, but I did it and I'm still doing it.

Any runner will tell you that building stamina and endurance takes discipline. You've got to have an unrelenting dedication to lacing up the sneakers nearly every day and hitting the pavement. You could limit your growth as an athlete without discipline. Practicing discipline is a mindset too. You have to decide that through hot or cold, rain or sun, you are going to get it in. When your schedule changes for one reason or another, you cannot see that as your lucky chance to escape your responsibility. Discipline dictates you keep it moving and you find alternate ways to get your miles in, even if it means using a bike or going out at a later time. Discipline also pushes you to find alternate ways to build strength and endurance, like weight training. In business, discipline is critical to getting things off the ground, growing and meeting goals in the business. Because there are so many components to starting a business, you must have discipline. As much as I love being an entrepreneur, I also have certain aspects to my business that I don't enjoy so much. I could choose to ignore those aspects and end up in trouble with the business, but discipline helps me keep focused on what needs to be done, whether it's my favorite part or not.

Runners also need a measure of self-motivation in order to get out there and make strides. Sure, it's nice to get accolades from well-wishers and loved ones, and it's nice to have incentives in place, but for me...self-motivation was a key factor in being able to be consistent in getting up in the morning and getting out there before the start of my work day. Because I was not affiliated with any running organizations or groups, self-motivation was what drove me to keep doing it day after day. And I would add that entrepreneurs must also be self-motivated. There are no bosses over you telling you what to do or how to do it. You may have advisors or investors, but ultimately, you are the driver of your business and you determine what needs to happen. Your motivation may be the difference between getting paid or not.

Take note of the relationship between these factors: Clear vision, fearlessness, risk-taker, discipline, and self-motivation. They all feed into the kind of drive and determination you must have to "Make it Happen". They also cross into other fields of interest. They are not limited to running or starting a business. They have cross appeal if you are interested in launching a new career, going back to school, writing a book, or changing your lifestyle. These factors speak to how badly you want something. You cannot just have a passing fancy to do something new, because you may experience tough times. If you are doing what you are destined to do, it will be easier to have the drive and determination needed to overcome those tough times.

When you are walking outside of your purpose, you may find that for the larger percentage of your time, you are not fulfilled. That's why I don't recommend doing something new and different just because it looks cool or looks like fun, but rather because you know it's what you're supposed to be doing. When you are walking in purpose, you don't give up readily when the going gets tough and things aren't going the way you want them to go. You have a sticktuitiveness that overrules the frustrations of things not going well. This is what true drive and determination look like.

I should caution you about too much drive and determination because it can also have adverse effects for you if you do not establish balance in your life. Driven people can have a "one track mind" and get completely engrossed in what they are trying to do. It's especially true for entrepreneurs. I've been guilty of this at times. It is easy for me to work 15 hour days and not feel it in terms of stress or fatigue, because I am driven. I could easily get lost in my work, almost like an obsession, if I am not careful. I can become consumed with new ideas and forget there is life outside of my passions. Because I am very ambitious, I want to get things done in no time flat, which is why it is so easy for me to keep working well into the night and ignore the need for balance. Living without balance is not healthy for your relationships and overall well-being. Balance entails leaving time for family, friends, and for yourself to breathe and enjoy life. Without balance, you could burn out, become more susceptible to illness, push away loved ones, or lose creativity. The mind operates more efficiently and with greater innovation in a relaxed state.

If you are looking to become more driven and determined, you have to be willing to act as though your life depended on your drive. Sometimes you need a sense of urgency to get things done. That might mean creating deadlines that are not negotiable. I do it all the time. I have a tendency to put off tasks until the last minute and with the help of my assistant, I've been doing a much better job planning and scheduling tasks. However as I was writing this book, I found myself putting off sitting down to write. I would make excuses like I didn't have enough of a time block to really make a dent in the writing or I would edit a million times. What I found was that I was not making the kind of progress I needed to make. So I put a deadline in place. I scheduled a book launch, brought an editor onto my team and then all of a sudden, my drive kicked in. I had to get rid of the excuses and get to work! Now others were depending on me to complete the book and I didn't have time to waste.

You may also find that as you are fighting to make yourself more driven and determined, you may need help. Don't be afraid to find models who have succeeded in what you would like to do and follow their example. Who can you talk to who will push you, hold you accountable or cheer you on as you pursue your dreams? Sometimes others make the difference and can change your own inner motivation and drive. Do what you have to do to "Make it Happen" in your life, business or career.

**Tonya's Take Aways**
**Whenever you seek to do something new in your life, business or career, you are faced with many decisions, including the obvious decision to accomplish what you set out to achieve. Many obstacles and barriers may try to interrupt your journey, but you have to be dedicated and committed to seeing success. You have to get rid of the excuses,**

discipline yourself and keep moving until you have reached your destination. The end result will be fulfillment and an overwhelming sense of accomplishment. Do not quit, be determined.

# 7 DEVELOP A PLAN

"Where are we going?" I asked my husband. He seemed to be going in circles, driving aimlessly through the DC streets, left turn, right turn, another left, another right, it was ridiculous. We were in Washington, DC spending time with our son in college. After leaving his campus, we were going to drive to Maryland to stay with friends. I turned on the GPS because I knew we would need it, but my husband insisted that he knew where we were going and so he ignored every turn he was supposed to make and kept going towards what he thought was the right direction. It wasn't. He wanted me to shush the GPS and trust him. I wanted to trust him. He had lived in DC for a number of years himself, but my instincts told me differently. He was very determined to find his way, but he didn't have a real plan for how to get to his destination. Had he had a true plan or a map that he followed, the ride might have been more pleasant and shorter. I just felt that we were wandering around in all different directions, with the GPS trying to reroute and take us in the right direction. He was so far off course, he wasted gas and it took us double the time to get to our destination. In this case, his determination was more detrimental than helpful.

I should not be surprised that we were so far off course, we didn't use our roadmap for the journey. Whenever you set out on a journey, you need to know where you are going. The same holds true for launching a business, new career or doing something new in your life. You need a roadmap or a plan of action to stay the course. The plan can be formal or informal, but you need to have an idea of the direction you are going to take so that you do not get lost and start wandering around wasting precious time. This leads me to the **5<sup>th</sup> Principle, which is to Develop A Plan.**

When I first started my business, I didn't have a plan. I just had an idea of what I wanted to do. In fact, I had a lot of ideas. I attempted to plan my ideas, but I didn't really know how to narrow them. I started out trying to work two or three different businesses at one time. A typical day consisted of me doing more than any one person could realistically do at one time. I was building websites, writing books, balancing checkbooks, trying to acquire new clients, I founded non-profits as well as my for-profits, and I ended everyday feeling like I accomplished little to nothing. I had no real direction as to which way I was going and I wondered why I wasn't doing well. Don't get me wrong, I was busy, very busy, but I was not making any progress nor did I have a clear vision of what I wanted to do with my business. Even when I did get a new client, I didn't have a standard service I provided, I did whatever they wanted me to do, whether I was an expert or not. I was just happy to get a client. I was willing to put in the time to prepare myself for the task and sometimes the time was very lengthy. This approach to owning a business is not one that I highly recommend. It was ineffective, to say the least.

I remember talking to my husband one day, frustrated and lost, "I don't know what I want to do. I feel I'm all over the place and no place at all." I shared with him how I felt like I was riding around without a map. I didn't have a plan. I didn't have a mission. I didn't know what was most important to me. I did not have goals or objectives and I certainly didn't have much to show for my long meaningless work days.

At one point I put together a summer program for children (at the prompting of friends). The program was a literacy program that also had an arts component. It was set up somewhat like a summer camp program, without the sports. I had a group of children who signed up for it, but it ultimately failed from a business perspective. It really had potential to be an excellent, model program, but I didn't have enough students to financially sustain the program. I had to make the tough decision to shut the program down early because I couldn't pay my staff. I felt horribly and took full responsibility for the failure. I was very disappointed in myself for not planning well in advance for the program. I was more concerned with disappointing people because they were depending on me to provide a safe, enriching environment for their children. Needless to say, that was a tough summer for me. I learned a lot from my mistakes, but the biggest lesson learned was the lesson that I have to plan for everything, otherwise, I will get into trouble.

After shutting down the program, I moped around for a little while, but realized I needed to let my lessons compel me to act differently moving forward. I needed help. So I started researching. Alan Lakein, a well-known author on time management said this, *"Failing to plan is planning to fail."* Ouch! That was my problem all the way. I learned that there was a lot I didn't know that I didn't know. How to effectively plan for my business was one of those things I didn't know. I thought because I had great ideas and a strong career background, that would make me successful. It's not enough to just have a dream. You need a plan to bring the dream to fruition.

Imagine you have a dream to launch a music career and you decide to start recording yourself and putting up videos online for others to enjoy. You start to get a little following and it's growing each week after you post new videos. You're actually very talented and people enjoy hearing you sing. However, you are only getting traction online. So far, you've made $0 singing. What's your plan? How do you plan to turn your talent into revenue? Will you record a full project to sell online? How will you market yourself? How will you get the funds to pay for the recording, post-production, manufacturing, marketing and promotion? Will you take a tour? How long will it take you? Where will you go to promote the project? How much will it cost? How many sales do you anticipate making and will they cover your costs? Who will help you with the production, marketing and sales and live performances? There is a lot for you to consider when launching your new independent singing career. Simply being a good singer is not enough. How will you handle it if you are an overnight success and in great demand around the world? You need a plan! You need to know how you will make your dreams come true in a strategic way that lets you have some control over the process.

At the beginning of the book, we spent some time exploring your vision for your dream. Hopefully you took the time to write your vision down. If not, I highly recommend you close the book and take some time to write down your vision. What do you envision yourself doing by this time next year? What about in three or five years? Do you have a picture in your mind? That's a great place to start. Two well-known educational experts, Grant Wiggins & Jay McTighe recommend educators plan with the end in mind and then work backwards to "Make it Happen".

That approach can be done with anybody. If you carefully create the vision of what you'd like to see happen in your life, business or career in the next 3-5 years, then you can work backwards to put elements in place to help you along the way. It's similar to taking a long road trip. Before taking the trip, you spend time mapping it out, checking off points along the way to sightsee, do adventures, shop, sleep and eat. You measure out how long it will take you, how much gas you'll need and how much you're eating and leisure stops will cost you. Once you do this, you have an idea of what to bring with you. You are now ready to take your trip. You've started with the trip and then worked your way backwards.

Keeping the end in mind helps you to be strategic in your planning and helps you to focus and be more productive. Writing out your plan allows you to flesh out the details, anticipate the problems and create solutions.

Currently, I am helping my church with strategic planning. We are not a new church, but we'd like to make some changes and plan for our next 3-5 years. During our first meeting with the team, we did a SWOT analysis. That's when we look at the organization internally for its strengths and weaknesses and externally for its opportunities and threats. After going through the analysis, we realized there were some values that were very obvious to us that will feed our long and short term planning.

What if you did a personal SWOT analysis and really looked deep within to see what is most important to you? You may want to ask another trusted individual, like your accountability partner to engage with you in dialog about the process. What does your SWOT reveal about you? (**The Fight to Make it Happen Handbook** has an analysis chart for you to complete, but I am also including it here for your benefit. Note the key questions to guide your analysis.)

| Strengths | Weaknesses |
|---|---|
| · What advantages do you have?<br><br>· What do you do exceptionally well?<br><br>· What do others see as your strengths? | · What could you do better?<br><br>· What are you criticized for or receive complaints about?<br><br>· Where are you vulnerable? |
| Opportunities | Threats |
| · What opportunities do you know about but haven't pursued?<br><br>· Are there other opportunities that you can pursue? | · What external roadblocks are there that could block your progress?<br><br>· Are there any financial evidences affecting your ability to progress?<br><br>· Is there any significant change coming that could affect your progress? |

Your strengths will probably reveal those things that you are good at doing, things you are passionate about as well as your values. Your weaknesses will require that you are honest with yourself about the things you are not good at doing or the things that do not come naturally for you or are difficult for you. You might be surprised to see that your values also come out in your weaknesses. The things you are not good at may be things that are very important to you.

Why do you think knowing your values is relevant to the planning process? Because I don't want you wasting your time on things that are not important to you.

Continue with the analysis and list all of the potential opportunities that you can take advantage of over time. Think outside the box. Are there any possibilities that you may not have explored or considered? Are there organizations or individuals who could help you or partner with you as you develop your long term plan? What are the external threats? What could potentially stop you from moving forward? Or slow down your progress? If you can anticipate what could possibly threaten your ability to reach your dreams, you empower yourself. Knowing your opportunities could open doors for you and knowing your threats could help you put plans in place to work around them.

After you've gone through this exercise, you should have more clarity on what you're supposed to be doing and where you may need some help. For example, if you are a great writer but have trouble with follow through, you may find that you need to put a strategy in place for how you will write and complete your book or series of books. You will need an accountability partner or rigid dates on the calendar where others will be expecting a product from you.

Planning for your future can be both exciting and overwhelming. For one, the process is not usually one that you can rush through in a few minutes to complete. The depth of your plan will make the difference in how you proceed. I confess that the times I haven't planned well were most detrimental. The times I plan well, I get things done. Your plans should also be detailed and specific. This can be tedious. If this is not a strength of yours, solicit help from someone who complements your weaknesses.

Once you're ready to sit down and begin the planning process, gather the necessary information, data, resources, tools, etc. that you may need. For example, if your dream is to go back to school and get your Master's degree, you'll need a calendar, computer or pen/paper, information about the schools of interest, costs to enter, dates of application, financial aid information (if applicable) or job reimbursement information, required testing information, letters of recommendation, and any new information you learned from your SWOT analysis. Your planning tools or resources are going to depend on what you would like to plan.

Don't disregard the importance of planning for your future. A plan can be the bridge from your dreams to fulfillment. The better your plan, the less guessing you have to do along the way. While you are planning you have the option of planning for change, growth, the unexpected, for rainy days, etc. You decide what you want to include in your plans. Your plan can also change over time. You should see it as a living document, meaning you can make changes along the journey as you see fit. You may find that there are opportunities that come your way that you didn't anticipate during your SWOT analysis, but they are in line with your values and goals, and may get you to your destination sooner than planned. Remain open minded and never see your plan as inflexible.

Now that you've done your SWOT analysis and drafted a vision for your future, let's take it a step further. We spent a lot of time earlier in the book talking about your purpose, which I call your "why". Your purpose can also be equated to your mission. Your mission can be broken down into a simple statement like mine, "Help Others Succeed." I've seen longer, more detailed mission statements, so feel free to develop one that is representative of you. Organizations always have mission statements, but it's less common for individuals to have mission statements, but I think this helps you stay focused throughout your planning process. Your personal mission statement can be very powerful. The mission should be aligned to your values, those qualities that are most important to you. Play around with a few ideas and then ask people what they think. You can test market it with those you trust. If you are looking to apply for a new job or launch a new career, you may choose to include your mission statement on your resume to give the potential employer an idea of who you are, what is important to you and what you stand for.

Now that you've created your mission statement, think about what the statement says about you. Is it a good reflection of what you want to do, how you want to do it and what makes you valuable? Does your mission statement define you? Does it correlate to what you envision for your future? If your dream is to move up in your company to a leadership position, how does your mission statement reflect that? Is there some mention of leadership qualities or characteristics and your aspirations to move up? Take the time needed to develop a sound mission statement that accurately reflects you.

Now that you have an idea of what you would like to see happen, you are ready to get into the planning process. This phase takes more time creating than a mission statement because you are going to work from the end (3-5 years from now) backwards to today. That's not easy.

My husband and I have been involved in helping people maintain healthy marriages or many years and we have held three marriage conferences and participated in planning others affiliated with our church. Planning for these conferences were very involved. We were fortunate to have other people on our team working with us, but the process of planning was still somewhat arduous. I have to admit, I enjoy the execution phase far greater than the planning phase, but if you don't plan well, there will be little to execute.

Because we've been doing this for several years, we already had an established mission statement. We just needed to get into the meat of the planning. We needed goals, strategies to reach those goals, action steps with individual assignments and we needed to be able to measure our progress. Sound simple? Not necessarily. We had to have a clear picture in our heads of what we wanted to see by the day of the event and then we had to plot out the steps along the way to get us there. We had to know what we wanted to accomplish overall...in other words, what will people be able to walk away with after they attend our conference? That helped us narrow our goals/objectives. I'm going to use goals/objectives interchangeably, although there is an argument that they can be separated, like in the field of education. Teachers wrote objectives for students that were specific. These objectives were included in lesson plans weekly. However, since you are not necessarily a teacher, I will use both words interchangeably.

We had to ask ourselves questions like, "When our guests leave the conference, what will they be able to do differently?" This was a great starting point for us because we were planning for an event. You may need to ask yourself different questions about what you expect to be able to accomplish in the time that you've allotted. After you've done that, try writing your goals/objectives. For example:

- ☐ By the end of 3 years, I will be able to use my Law Degree to represent indigent citizens in my county.
- ☐ By the end of 3 years, my new business will become the local go-to organization for human resources outsourcing with over $1 million in revenue.
- ☐ By the end of 3 years, I will be a recognized author and public speaker, speaking 3-5 times/weekly.

Do you get the idea? Notice how these goals are considered **SMART**, meaning they are **S**pecific, **M**easurable, **A**ttainable, **R**elevant, and **T**ime-Bound? Make sure you set goals that are precise and can be measured along the way. Even though you might be very ambitious, make sure you can reach the goals you set for yourself. It would be unrealistic to think you can write a book to be used as a textbook for a college course in a month's time. Make sure that what you set as a goal is aligned to your mission and values. Avoid creating goals that are interesting or enjoyable, but not aligned to your mission and values. If you find that your goals are not aligned, go back and see what's missing in your SWOT, what's missing in your mission and what's missing in your values. The point of planning strategically is so that you are not all over the place or lost in achieving your ultimate vision. You should see alignment in everything you plan.

Because you now have the end picture in mind, you can develop the plan that will help you accomplish your goals. You may choose to use a strategy like creating a timeline with your milestone accomplishments scattered throughout your designated time periods. You may rather decide to answer certain questions like:

- ☐ How do I reach my goals?
- ☐ What needs to happen to meet my goals?
- ☐ Who needs to be involved in helping me accomplish my goals?
- ☐ What changes in my routine need to be made?
- ☐ Where can I go for help?
- ☐ What costs are associated with my journey? How will I get the funds?
- ☐ Which goals are most important? Do they build upon another? Which goals get priority?
- ☐ Is there a sense of urgency about accomplishing certain goals?
- ☐ What other resources do I need to attain my goals?

Consider a 30-60-90 day goal breakdown as a strategy. This might help you get some items off of your plate, prioritize those things that are most urgent and begin the process. Once you've answered the questions that are relevant for your dreams, decide on the specific actions that need to take place and the timeline for each. And if there are others who will help you, match them to their action steps and give them a time frame as well. Review every action step and determine if you can indeed follow your timeline and get each action accomplished. Keep in mind that the action steps must include every minor detail.

Once you are settled on the path you will take, you need to put metrics in place to assess where you are at different points of the journey. Can you check in with someone (like your accountability partner) at different points to share how you've made certain accomplishments and determine if your course of action is still effective and working for you? If not, you may need to decide how to restructure your plan to accommodate your changing vision or timeframe. How will you measure your success? If you opened a new business, you may choose to look at how many clients you've attained and the amount of revenue from each client/customer or how many regions you've been able to serve. If you are training to become a doctor, your grades and evaluations may be a measurement you use to assess your progress. How you measure progress will vary based upon your goals and aspirations. Essentially you need to be able to measure whether you are succeeding at achieving your goals. If you are, you are well on your way to living your dreams.

I hope you see the value of planning out how to reach your

dreams. Why should your dreams be fulfilled accidentally or haphazardly? If you don't plan, you run the risk of taking a very long time to reach your goals or worse, never reaching them at all. You cannot predict everything that comes your way on your journey, but you can lessen the challenges by planning for them. Journeys are not as fun without a roadmap, otherwise it's an adventure. Adventures can be fun, but they can also keep you from reaching your destination.

**Tonya's Take Aways:**
**The time you take to sit down and map out your dream journey is worth it. It keeps you from getting lost, distracted or taken off course. Planning doesn't eliminate detours that cause you to be rerouted from time to time, but because you know where you are going, you can get back on the main road in no time at all. Plan carefully, plan well, your future depends upon it.**

# 8 FIGHT!

"I might be down, but I'm not beat!" Words spoken by a very close friend of mine, suffering with a serious illness. I referenced her in the chapter about drive and determination as my inspiration for running. She's not my inspiration just because she runs in spite of her illness. She is my inspiration because she fights every day to keep moving even against the odds that from time to time one side of her body might get numb and tingly or her vision might start playing tricks on her or worse, she may need to have to make periodic visits and stays in the hospital. She literally runs because it is her peace in the storm, her refuge from the pain and turmoil of her disease and because it makes her stronger to fight! Her life depends on her fight! **Fight is our 6th and final Principle.**

Most of us are fortunate that we are not in the midst of a fight for our lives, but we still must tap into that fight from time to time when things aren't going the way we want them to go in our lives, careers or businesses. Have you ever had to fight for your dreams? Have you ever had to go to battle for your dreams? Have you ever had to combat something or someone to be able to go after your dreams? If your answer is no, keep living. At some point on your journey, you may need to rally the fighter in you to keep you moving and keep you from retreating, abandoning or giving up on your dreams. If you've had to fight, this chapter may resonate with you and serve as an encouragement to you.

The truth is, when I chose to go after my dreams of becoming an entrepreneur, I was setting myself up for some days that were going to be up and other days that were going to be down. I knew this going in. I was not blind to the fact that not everything will go my way just because I own my own business. I was aware and usually very optimistic. Earlier in the book I shared a very personal story about my house going into foreclosure and how I had to use my faith to help me get through that challenge. It was a very emotional story to experience and tell. Even as I wrote about it, I found myself reliving the moment and I could feel the tears welling up inside of me. This is an example of where I had to fight. I had to fight my fears, my despair, my inner voices that told me to surrender and the reality that I wasn't making enough money.

At this point in my entrepreneurial journey, I had good reason to leave and go back to work for somebody else. Some might have advised me to do this, but I didn't seek any advice, intentionally. I didn't want to hear anything that would confirm my fears or suggest that I failed. I already knew that I was failing. The difference for me was that my failings were not going to define me. I was not a failure! I fought any urge to flirt with that idea. I understood the facts, which were that my company was not bringing in enough revenue to help me pay my bills and as a result, my home was in active foreclosure. That was a fact, but that fact was not going to be my story. I am an overcomer! My faith kicked in like never before and I had to begin to believe that this was temporary, I would be able to turn this around and I would learn from my mistakes and keep it moving.

My fight was a fight of the mindset! I could not allow my circumstances to derail what I had been trying to build since inception. I had to use my biggest weapon and that was my faith. Plato said, *"We are twice armed if we fight with faith."* Fighting with my faith meant that I had to see something that didn't yet exist. I had to have hope in spite of what the reality and facts were. I knew the facts. I knew the reality. But I also knew the power of faith and like Plato said, I was doubly armed with my faith.

I could not wallow in my sorrow and I could not continue to have a pity party. There was no victory in either of those. Sure, I could have gone back to work, but I was in the middle of a battle and needed to win. So what did I do? I allowed my faith to convince me that I would get out of this and that I would eventually get a modification from my mortgage company, even though I had been denied. I didn't have any support for this belief, but I continued to believe it and took action. Remember I told you that your faith must be accompanied with action to prove you really have faith? Well that's what I did. I combined the two and added changing my speech as well. I spoke in faith, meaning I would not let defeating thoughts come out of my mouth. When I was a little girl, my grandmother would tell me, "Words are things, watch what you let come out of your mouth. It could come true." She believed in the power of words and the weight they carried in one's life. So I only spoke of those things that were positive, hopeful and optimistic.

I was not delusional. I knew the facts, but the facts were not going to be what drove me. I only allowed the positive to drive me. I guarded myself with my weapon of faith and my protective shield of action. Together, these two made me a powerful warrior against my circumstances. I surrounded myself with positivity as well, feeding my mind with books and words that were motivational, encouraging, and uplifting and I took action. I started creating new ideas that would bring in revenue, like starting a tutoring service. I boosted my performance to drum up consulting business and stepped outside of my comfort zone by making cold calls. I increased my marketing activities and constantly sought more ideas for how I could improve on my efforts. What happened after that was a first for me. Opportunities became available to me and some seemed out of nowhere. It was a little odd, but also amazing. I learned something that would later repeat itself many times in the coming years. I learned that when I go to work and build momentum, things happen in my favor. I was planting seeds and started reaping a harvest, sometimes the harvest came when I didn't expect it and other times it would come directly after I planted a seed. There were times that the clients would come from efforts that were made much earlier from the start of the business. The point is...a harvest eventually came as a result of my efforts. Planting seeds were critical. The biggest lesson for me was to keep moving in spite of what I saw because I would reap what I sowed, eventually.

Had I not fought the fight with faith, what might have happened to me? I don't usually sit around speculating of what could have happened, but for the purposes of this book, I thought there might be some value in allowing my mind to think through the possibilities without lingering there. There is value in thinking through the "what if" process. It could bring clarity to you. I could have chosen to go back into the school system full time again, but my heart would not have been in it. If that had been the case, the students would not have gotten the best from me and therefore I would have compromised the quality of their educational experiences. If I had gone back into the school system, my financial situation would have turned around, but I would not have been fully invested mentally which could have caused stress and anxiety. Stress and anxiety lead to health challenges. If I had gone back into the school system, I would have essentially been allowing my dreams to die and I don't know if I would have had the drive to try again. My husband may have likely put pressure on me to stay put so that we didn't run the risk of ruining our credit again. If I had gone back, I would not know what it is to learn from my failure, grow from my failure and turn around my business and put it back on the path to success. Sometimes you have to trust your instincts and keep it moving.

I could have chosen to seek the counsel of others and I'm sure there may have been some people who might have advised me against continuing on this entrepreneurial journey. They might have said things like, "This is a sign that you're not supposed to be an entrepreneur." Or "Maybe you should consider going back to work. You are a very good educator; I'm sure you won't have any trouble getting hired." I know that if these words were spoken to me, the deliverer of the messages would be well meaning, but not in line with my strong faith. That's the very reason I didn't seek it.

You may encounter your own kind of fight, but I want you to be prepared to combat it when you are faced with it. I don't want you to be deceived that everything will be perfect when you start your journey towards living your dreams. I wish I could guarantee that for you, but I do not have that authority. Obstacles and barriers are almost expected to come before you at some point or another. How you decide to handle it will make the difference in the outcomes and how much they affect you. Sometimes you can anticipate the kinds of challenges that may come your way and prepare yourself for the battle. You can begin to train yourself before the fight begins.

Have you ever watched a boxing match? When I was growing up, my father would watch different boxing matches. I would often watch with him. I was a big Sugar Ray Leonard fan. (I'm dating myself here.) I confess to having a school girl crush on him, which might explain why I often watched him fight. One thing that was obvious in a boxing match was that the winner was not only the better fighter, but the most prepared. To be the most prepared involved training and the training entailed learning how to anticipate what the opponent might do in the ring so that he could avoid getting hurt. To be successful in a boxing match, the boxer needed to be more on the offense than the defense. He needed to be able to block his opponent, duck his opponent's punches and ultimately be left as the last man standing or the one who fought the better fight, if there is no knock out at the end.

The boxing matches were divided into 3 minute rounds and could last for up to 12 total rounds, which meant the boxer had to exercise more stamina and endurance. You too must be prepared for what might be ahead. You will need stamina and endurance when you are going after your dreams because they may take longer than you expect. Like boxers, you can anticipate some of the jabs that might be thrown at you. In other words, you can expect things to happen in your life that could take you off your game and steer your attention away from your pursuit of your dreams. And when this happens, you need to be prepared with a plan for what you are going to do. How are you going to handle it? Will you fall apart? No! You will fight! You will do whatever it takes to make your dreams come true.

While you are pursuing your dreams, expect things to change along the way. Expect your plans to be impacted in some way. Like the boxer, train for these possibilities. Lean on others who can help you, encourage you and push you. Remember the importance of building strong relationships. These relationships could be life-saving when you are up against the biggest odds. Just make sure you prepare yourself so that you don't lose the fight. And although you cannot predict what could go wrong, you could prepare for some things going wrong. Some things may be outside of your control, while other things may be within your control. For example, you may make a wrong decision that causes your plans to be altered or stalled. You may lose out on opportunities that you seek. You may experience a sudden personal or family illness.

You may lose a loved one. You may run out of resources. Your support system may leave you to attend to their own personal matters. You may have doors closed on you that you were expecting to be open. You may get other (non-related) opportunities that detract your attention from your dreams. You may get discouraged along the way because it's taking too long for you to see your dreams come true. You may run into apparent insurmountable barriers that stop you from moving forward. And if any of these things happen to you, what are you going to do? How are you going to refocus yourself, address your needs, lift your spirits, bounce back and pick yourself up again? You have to fight! You have to push yourself beyond what you may be accustomed to pushing, but NEVER give up the fight! This is your life! This is your destiny!

Are there times that you may need to evaluate where you are and start over? Sure, that may happen from time to time. In fact, be aware of how and why you allow yourself to get completely off track. Ask yourself whether the path you are on is really the path you should be on or whether the circumstances in your life changed because your path is also supposed to change. Sometimes we are supposed to heed the situations that come into our lives because they are meant to lead us down another road towards our dreams. It's even possible that the change in your circumstances could be for a bigger and better reason. I didn't remain a beauty consultant forever, although that would have been my sales director's preference. At some point, that part of my journey was over. The circumstances that led to that era ending were not anticipated, but all signs showed me that my season as a beauty consultant was over and it was time for me to move on to new things.

I was not able to see in the moment all that I am able to see now, but what became clear to me was that I no longer needed to be involved in that business. I received from it what I was supposed to get and that was the confidence to be able to speak publicly. I was never supposed to remain in that company. If I had remained, it would have detracted me from what was ahead for me. Only hindsight can give me such clarity. I have no regrets as a result.

So that's why it is important to pay attention to the reason why you are doing what you are doing and whether or not it really is supposed to be a permanent situation for you or something with an expiration date. Sometimes you need to make changes, drastic changes. Don't fight the necessary changes that may need to happen in your life for you to keep moving and growing into the person you were designed to become.

There is a brighter side to when things go wrong, you can be prepared for them. You don't have to be taken completely off track. You can plan for some potential roadblocks and barriers. Sometimes that plan may include financial planning, as in putting away money in the event that you need it. You may be able to train someone else to take over your responsibilities in the event that you are not able or capable of carrying out your normal duties because you may have to absent yourself for a period of time. Doing this may keep your dream from dying while you are handling other matters. You may be able to anticipate challenges that could potentially come your way and put plans in place ahead of time to address these challenges. You might recall, I had to stop going to graduate school temporarily when I had my car accident. However, I knew deep down inside that I needed that advanced degree in order for me to be qualified for my next stop on this journey, so I notified the school and asked them about rejoining the program at a later date. I didn't know when that date would be, but I was able to rejoin.

Fighting for your dreams may require incredible strength and will power, depending on how much you are facing in terms of adversity. No one is a superhuman and adversity can evoke a lot of strong emotions. When I had to shut down my summer program for lack of funds, I realized I had made a huge mistake. I went through a few months of feeling pretty low in terms of my energy levels and morale. I wouldn't say I was depressed, but I would say I was discouraged. I'll never forget being approached by a friend during the weeks that followed the summer failure. "Tonya, are you okay, you haven't seemed like yourself lately?" I responded that I was fine, BUT I knew that I wasn't. I thought I had been doing a good job masking my emotions by painting on a smile and continuing as I had been, but I wasn't okay. I had to fight back tears trying to keep a straight face and upbeat attitude as I weaseled my way out of telling her what was going on.

I didn't quite know how to explain that things weren't going so well for my business. I wasn't succeeding. Business was at a standstill and I was not able to pay myself anything. I was not accustomed to not succeeding and I certainly didn't want others to know that I was not succeeding. I had never been in this position before and wasn't handling it too well. I made up an excuse for why I wasn't myself and tried to convince her and myself that I was just a little tired, overworked or something that seemed to get me out of having to expose the reality that I was failing. She seemed to buy my lame excuses or at least she didn't keep asking questions and I escaped any potential judgment. This mask was not working for me. Plus, I was not even tapping into the support network that was around me. She could have been a support, but I internalized everything and tried to keep it to myself. I missed a very valuable opportunity. I realized I needed help.

Sometimes in the midst of your greatest challenges, you may need help. And help is available, if you are willing to swallow your pride long enough to seek it. I had to do just that. I had to face myself in the mirror and be honest with what I was seeing happening to myself. I was not satisfied with the reflection and so I sought help and I found it too. Again, let me remind you of the importance of strong relationships. These relationships can help you through the challenges that come your way. You do not have to go it alone. And you can probably ascertain from my story that going it alone did not help me.

The biggest lesson I learned after this failure was that I had a lot to learn. Just because I had been a successful educator doesn't translate to me being a successful business owner. I didn't become a successful educator overnight, I received training, continual training. I had models and mentors to follow and of course I had drive and determination. When I became a business owner, I jumped into it without having received any training whatsoever. I hadn't even read any business books. I didn't have a mentor nor any models that I was following. No wonder I failed! I needed professional development. My industry knowledge was not enough for me to have a successful business. I needed business knowledge to complement the industry expertise. The eye opening realization changed everything for me. I was finally awake and the fighter in me rose. I put on my boxing gloves and I went into the ring.

My first round was equipping myself by reading everything I could lay my hands on. I started listening to books through my Audible.com app on my phone as I was exercising, walking, cleaning, riding in my car. I became hungry for information. I got rid of all excuses. I was now inspired and I had my drive back. It seems that when I get into my fight mode, things start to happen for me. I start to build momentum and I am fierce! Round 2 - I found a free online conference for women business owners and I signed up for it. It was an all-day marathon of speakers, one after the other from morning until evening and it was awesome. I heard things I had never heard before and I knew that I could turn my business around. If all of these women could build successful businesses, I could too. This was the beginning of my development process. I also invited my accountability partner to tune into the conference so that we could share and bounce ideas off of one another at the end of the conference. It was very helpful. But I didn't stop there, I moved on to Round 3 – where I later found another full day conference for small businesses in my local area where I was able to gain more helpful information. I attended and met other small business owners who were at different stages of building their businesses. This gave me an opportunity to network. I knew that I was not alone.

The rounds kept on moving and I was gaining ground, restructuring and making changes, lots of changes in my business. I joined a Christian Chamber of Commerce and later a local group with other Women Business Owners and I started developing a network of other business owners who could support me and I could support them. I was getting my legs! I kept on fighting...fighting for the win at the end of the match! I would win some and lose some, but I kept on fighting. I wish every decision after that was always right for me, but it wasn't. But I never lost sight of the goals again...the goal to win the Championship...which for me is be in a position to not only replace my former salary as a principal, but also be able to start and fund a non-profit organization as well. I still have more rounds to fight, but I will keep on training and keep on fighting. Each time I fight, I learn something new about myself, my industry or my business. I am on a roll! I will not quit! This means too much to me to give up.

I've learned that no obstacle is too big, no hurdle is too high and no opponent is too quick or strong for me. When I keep fighting, I not only develop, but I inspire others to do the same. Anybody can fight with the right frame of mind and the right people in your corner training, mentoring and supporting you. When you fight for your dreams, you prove the naysayers wrong, you quiet the critical remarks, you overcome fears and doubts, you remove negativity and you will see the success that you are working towards. And when you reach your dreams, reach higher for new dreams. Don't just climb the mountain, celebrate and then come back down to the bottom and be done forever. Find a new mountain to climb and fight your way up that new mountain until you are again victorious!

**Tonya's Take Aways:**

**Remember that your mindset is huge to your success. It's where the fighter in you is shaped and formed...in your mind. Your mindset needs to be fed with words of encouragement, motivation, faith, patience, will-power, drive, and determination. Feed your mind daily so that you are equipped and prepared for the battles that lie ahead as you push to "Make it Happen" in your life, career or business. See failures as opportunities to learn and grow and never give up when the going gets tough. Build momentum by taking action and waiting for your seed time to bring about a harvest. You can do it – Don't give up! You can fight and you can win!**

# 9 WHAT'S NEXT?

This book is my most recent and best example of my *Fight to Make it Happen*. Writing this book for me is a dream come true, but I had a lot of distractions and interruptions. I almost didn't get it finished. The first record I found where I memorialized this dream to write a book is estimated to be from 2002 or 2003. I didn't have a journal, so I used loose pieces of paper to journal and I wrote about my desire to write a book. This was not my first time voicing my desire to write.

When I was a little girl, I wrote my first book. It has never been published. I was about 9 years old and it was about a girl who was adopted. I don't remember much else about the plot, but it was a serious venture for me. I believe I can find the manuscript for it in a box of childhood mementoes in the basement. When I was 9, I remember telling my parents that I wanted to be a writer. They took me seriously because they saw evidence of it. I've always enjoyed writing. They even bought me my first electric typewriter so that I could type my stories, rather than handwrite them. I loved my typewriter. I think it was blue.

As an adult, I've attempted to write numerous books on a variety of topics, one being about the hard choices professional mothers make regarding their role as both professional and mother. A few other attempts were focused on the topic of marriage matters. This is another area of passion for me...healthy marriages. I started a book for school improvement, detailing some of my own experiences as a principal. I started a parenting guidebook with keys to helping children become successful, however I never completed any of these. While I was serving as principal, I did successfully complete and publish a children's chapter book for young readers. That book, *Mykayla Mitchell Moves Away*, is about a 2nd grader's challenge with moving away and the fear of losing and making friends. You can find it on Amazon. I wrote it after dreaming about the plot and wanted to inspire the students in my school to read more. The children loved the book!

However, I had not yet fulfilled my dream of writing a book for an adult population. I'd written blog posts, articles and I've been journaling for the past decade or more. But still no book. What was I waiting for? I was missing something in my life. I had the dream, I'd had it for many years. I had faith that I could do it. I had supporters in my corner who would push me, hold me accountable, if I started the process. I was missing the three latter principles, until now. I didn't have the drive and dedication needed to write. I procrastinated, made excuses and never fully committed to making it happen. I didn't have a plan for my book and I wasn't fighting to "Make it Happen". I was in the way of seeing my own dreams come true. I think ultimately I wasn't ready yet to see my dream come true. The timing wasn't yet right.

When you are ready to make your dreams come true, you move. You take steps and you get the ball rolling, even if you don't yet have a plan. It's because the urge is so strong, you can no longer ignore it. No one can really force you to get started and quite honestly that doesn't make a lot of sense to me. If people have to force you to go after your own dreams, you aren't ready yet or they aren't your real dreams. People can encourage you or give you incentives like opening doors for you, but people cannot make you live your dreams. You have to want it. I asked this question earlier in the book, but it bears repeating, "How badly do you want it?"

It's very easy to keep living the status quo and never make changes in your life, but will you come to a point in your life when you look back and wish that you had started years earlier? Are you going to have regrets? Are you willing to live unfulfilled forever? Evaluate your life. Are you satisfied with it? Do you want more? Have you been wanting more in your life? Do you feel a calling or pulling of sorts to change your circumstances? Then pray about it, think about it, consider the consequences of **not** walking in purpose.

As you apply these 6 Power Principles to your life, understand that they do not necessarily work in a successive order. They are not steps to fulfilling your dreams, they are principles, so they may be working in tandem with one another and in different orders. You may find that it is better for you to dream it, plan it, and have faith that it can happen, before the other principles come into play. You may choose to start with the fight because of your life's experiences or your station in life. You may be one who needs to have faith first before you make any moves. Or you need to have others involved in your moving forward. I don't recommend you start with any one or two principles because everyone's story and situation is different and one size does not fit all. Just get started. Don't waste any more time.

People have been talking to me for years about what they wish they could do or what they want to do, but they are no closer today than they were years ago when they first told me about their desires. It's not enough for you to just have a wish. A wish is not a dream, nor is it action. You need more than a wish to start living your dreams. A wish may be a starting point, but if it doesn't go any further and develop into a dream and it's not connected to your purpose, it's pointless or ineffective.

The world is waiting for you to fulfill your purpose because purpose is connected to others. I believe God creates us with an intended purpose and that purpose is for the benefit of others. My purpose is to make a difference in the lives of others and help them succeed. Your purpose in life is something different, but will likely have an impact on others because we are relational people, dependent on one another. Remember, your purpose is your *"why," your mission in life.*

My writing this book, a long-standing dream of mine, is an opportunity for me to fulfill my *why,* my mission, my purpose. This book allows me to touch the lives of many and make a difference by helping others succeed. The dream of writing this book is very tangible and attainable. By now, I pray that you have discovered who you are while reading this book. I hope you figured out your *"why".* If not, I hope you have at least seriously started your journey to finding it.

I've identified the 6 Power Principles because they have guided my pursuit of my dreams and ultimate purpose. They have helped me believe that my dreams are attainable. They helped me align myself to the right people. They've helped me stay the course and not quit. They've helped me create a roadmap that leads to success and they are what I use to fight obstacles and barriers that block my success.

So now that you've read this book, now that you've become intimately familiar with these principles, what's next for you? How do you actually get started? First of all make a decision. I talked about making decisions all throughout this book because anything you do starts with a decision. You have to decide to start your journey towards living your dreams and fulfilling your purpose. Once you've made the decision to start, think about which of the 6 Power Principles you will use to get started. Your process for starting is unique to you and your comfort level. You may need to do some research before you decide what Principle makes sense for you. You may need to talk to someone before you get started. You may need to find models of success before you make any major decisions.

You might be scared and you might have a lot of uncertainties because you are doing something that has so much meaning and it's okay to have these feelings. I've had the same feelings at times. As I was writing this book, which by the way I've done in less than four months, I got very nervous at times. I knew in my gut that this would be the book that I actually finished and I knew that other people were going to read it. When I asked my brilliant friend to edit the book for me, I got even more nervous because I was now exposing my writing to her for major scrutiny and that was uncomfortable. I'm accustomed to doing things that don't require me to open myself up to criticism, albeit constructive, so this is kind of scary for me. But I know deep down that this is what I'm supposed to be doing. God has ordered my steps and paved the way for me to be able to do this, opening doors for me and the book to be a success. It's both exciting and scary, but I have faith and I believe God wants me to be successful.

So if you are venturing to do something you've never done before, don't allow fears to stop you from starting. Know that you are not alone and others would naturally feel the same way that you feel if they were in your shoes.

The following examples may give you some ideas for getting started with different dreams:

☐ If your dream is to run a marathon for the very first time, you've got to do some research about an appropriate training program, make sure you are cleared medically, get the right shoes and clothing, get running partners or coach or use an App like I did and get started.

☐ If your dream is to run for office, you will need to check with the local government offices for the requirements to getting on the ballot. You will need to complete the application process, raise funds, and rally support.

☐ If your dream is to travel the world in a year, you will need to first make sure you have a passport, financial resources to travel and make some decisions about how you will leave (Sell your home? Rent out your home? Take a sabbatical or quit your job?) and you'll need a plan for where you will go and stay.

- [ ] If your dream is to go to graduate school, you will need to have an idea about what you want to study and why, then research schools that offer your program of interest. Then you will need to follow the university's process for applying, which could include taking the GRE's, getting letters of recommendation, applying, of course and more.

- [ ] If your dream is to become an actor, you will need to decide whether you want to do theater, film or television acting. I recommend finding and taking classes in the area of acting where you have an interest. There you will be taught more about the industry and given further steps to take to audition for roles. You may also need other training like communication, singing, dancing, or public speaking.

- [ ] If your dream is to marry the man/woman of your dreams, I would recommend you work on your dating relationship first to make sure you have the components of a healthy relationship and then seek premarital counseling with a reputable counselor who will help you evaluate your relationship more in depth. You'll need to plan spiritually, financially and emotionally for the pending nuptials before taking the plunge.

☐ If your dream is to invest in real estate, you'll need to have access to resources, learn the industry, including the laws around buying and selling property, including tax responsibilities. You may opt to have partners in real estate. You'll also need to know the types of properties you want to make investments, whether you will flip your properties or hold onto them for rental profits. You'll need to decide on the location of properties as well.

---

Obviously, there are thousands more dreams you may want to pursue and each of them require different starting points, but all of them require action on your part. I cannot think of one dream that doesn't involve you doing something tangible to get started. Dreams do not come to life by remaining thoughts in your head. You cannot subliminally start living your dreams, you have to actively take a step. Sure some steps are bigger or more risky than the next one, but they are steps and you must take them. Take one step and then make plans for taking the second step. Each step you take will get you closer to your dreams. Once you've decided to take the first step, commit to it and put the 6 Power Principles into action. "Make it Happen!"

Let me also recommend you check out my mentoring programs on TonyaBreland.com or take the next six months to work through my **Fight to Make it Happen Handbook.**

You can work through it as an independent study or you can choose to work with me or a member of my team. Depending on when you are actually reading this book, I may have other programs in place to help you, but check out my website to see. I want to make sure that you are not alone through your journey, if that's not your preference.

The most important thing is that you get started living your dreams. Whenever I've had a dream to do something, I could not rest until I moved on it. It would play like a broken record in my head for as long as it took for me to take the necessary steps to "Make it Happen". I don't know if that happens to you or if there is something else that tells you there's more for you to do. I just hope that you will answer the call, the call to start living your dreams, the call to live a life of purpose. I want you to *Fight To Make it Happen*!

# ABOUT THE AUTHOR

Tonya hopes that readers have enjoyed reading this book. She is very passionate about helping others succeed. It is her mission to make a difference in the lives of others. Since the days of her youth, she has dedicated her life to doing this. Over the years she has impacted the lives of her peers, mentees, colleagues, staff, friends and family and at the heart of all of her interactions, she hopes that she has been able to add something positive and encouraging to help others feel valued, special and supported, like Mrs. Clark did for her.

Check out TonyaBreland.com or email her at Tonya@TonyaBreland.com for more information about how you can book Tonya as a Motivational Speaker, Educational Trainer or Mentor who helps individuals succeed.